Blessed Is the Day
We "Got It Wrong"

Costanza Miriano

BLESSED IS THE DAY WE "GOT IT WRONG"

A Guide to Marriage Renewal

SOPHIA INSTITUTE PRESS
Manchester, New Hampshire

Previously published in Italian under the title *Benedetto Il Giorno Che Abbiamo Sbagliato* © 2024 Sonzogno di Marsilio Editori® s.p.a. in Venezia

English translation © 2025 by Sophia Institute Press

Printed in the United States of America. All rights reserved.

Cover design and illustrations by Emma Helstrom.

Sophia Institute Press
Box 5284, Manchester, NH 03108
1-800-888-9344
www.SophiaInstitute.com

Sophia Institute Press® is a registered trademark of Sophia Institute.

paperback ISBN 979-8-88911-478-9
ebook ISBN 979-8-88911-479-6

Library of Congress Control Number: 2025938299

First printing

To Patricia Chendi – editor and friend –
who knew how to read both words and people,
uncovering the beauty in each,
even when it was tucked away quite deeply,
with affection and gratitude.
Who knows if in Heaven we'll finally have time
to chat about books, and boots, and the sea …

Contents

Blessed Is the Day
We "Got It Wrong"

Perfect Couples, Please Refrain

"**S**ure it's nice, but maybe you should start by saying that marriage isn't just a vale of tears, it's not the land of Mordor where Sauron ..."

All right, let me stop you right there, male friend who starts quoting *The Lord of the Rings*, because I haven't read it—I can never manage to bump it to the top of my pile. Yes, I know, I'm a disgrace to society; let me just say it myself, and I promise I'll fix it—or at worst I'll have it placed into my coffin. But please don't go further with that comparison, because then I can't follow you. Above all, I wasn't looking for advice; I only wanted compliments. But since you're a man, you think you need to fulfill some role, like offering a critical reading.

That said, I admit it: this book talks about marriages in which one of the spouses—or both—at a certain point (or at many points) feels the strain, or is touched by doubt, or is seized by the certainty of having made a mistake, tempted by the thought of an alternative, or else they're absolutely sure they want to stay but don't know how. They feel a certain lack that—spoiler alert—only the One who is greater can fill. After all, even His own disciples were shocked and said, "Then it's not worth it to marry at all." Every happy marriage I've ever encountered is like that, so imagine the unhappy ones—and there are some.

Blessed Is the Day We "Got It Wrong"

Surely your marriage is far above average, and this book probably isn't for you. I won't be offended; in fact, I'm happy for you. Of course you chose each other well, and yes, what you lack for complete fulfillment you know how to let God provide. But for everyone else, perhaps these pages can serve as a reminder that difficulty is never a deal-breaker; on the contrary, it's a call, a longing for completeness—a precious longing that reminds us to put our hearts in the right place, oriented toward the only One who heals, satisfies, and consoles. That's why we can say, "Blessed is the day we got it wrong," because every marriage is a set of circumstances in which we seek the totally Other, stepping outside ourselves, inconveniencing ourselves, accepting the conversion—small, bit by bit—demanded by that set of keys your husband leaves in a spot that drives you nuts, or your wife's smug Miss Perfect routine; not to mention the trash in the kitchen, on its way to becoming an art installation because none of the kids can manage to find in their packed schedules (chatting with friends, straightening their hair, playing PlayStation, glancing at Thucydides and X Factor) a three-minute window to throw it out—though negotiations are underway (the UN Secretary-General is expected any moment now).

Blessed is the day we got it wrong, because only by giving our lives to someone different from ourselves do we learn to love; it forces us to break ourselves open, to lose pieces along the way, bringing out a beauty that those who never give themselves away will never discover they have. Marriage saves us from ourselves, makes us move forward, and allows us to love—which is different from being in love.

All of which is to say that, yes, marriage isn't always a dark valley: I'm grateful to have married my husband, my irreplaceable, basic-model human being—the one with few extras (though, as

Henry Ford said, "What isn't there doesn't break"). He's the one who makes me cram everything I want to tell him in three hours into twelve seconds, because then he's out of the room, which teaches me to focus on the essentials. He's the one who gets annoyed at my absurd trips and grumbles but then makes sure the car has a full tank. While I change fourteen times because I have nothing to wear, he tells me fourteen times, "That's fine, but hurry up," without even raising his head from his book—he can't tell a turtleneck from a tank top (he only sees the "naked or dressed" option; that difference he does notice). He proudly wears impossibly old middle-school sweaters and fancy jackets with equal total disregard, because he's from Rome and knows that civilizations and people come and go, let alone their clothes (incidentally, he feels the bathrobe is an underrated casual outfit). Assuming he's listening at all, he never picks up on the tone of my voice, never knows if I'm angry or sad, has given up decoding me, and interrupts my mental contortions with, "Just tell me what I gotta do," thus saving me from myself countless times a day. He's the one who dampens my enthusiasm when I think I've given birth to children who'll leave an indelible mark on human history—Nobel and Pulitzer winners in the making—and curbs my slide into despair when I'm convinced that at best they'll become potato-peelers on the black market. He ignores our teenage daughters' tantrums, stopping them cold with one of his rare, adamant "no's," while using his favorite tactic with me: playing dead. He explains what Zionism is for the eight-thousandth time, with the same success (zero) I have when telling him why Francesca is in crisis with her husband. He lowers my self-esteem and criticizes me as freely as a brother would, but when necessary, he slips out those precious, painstakingly rationed words of appreciation—which I typically have engraved on bronze pendants and cherish for about a year (that's the frequency), because I know that on the rare occasions he says them, they're true.

So to him goes my most important thanks, because if he had been exactly how I wanted, I never would have become a woman.

Chapter Zero

Why Stay Married?

"**N**o, right now you need to explain why on earth I should stay married."

In reality, it's the universe that ought to explain to me why these questions always reach me at the worst possible moment in all of history—ever since the fall of the Roman Empire right up to today. Specifically, that moment when I'm biting into some kind of lunch (a protein bar I found in my purse that's stuck to a couple of hairs—just a few, and hopefully mine) while I'm trying to set up the GPS with a caramel-coated finger, so I can figure out where to pick up a cordial seventeen-year-old who sends me a message every twenty seconds asking, "Mooooom, why aren't you answering?!"

I'm not answering because I'm old, I can't see well, and—now that we're on the subject—I'm starting to have trouble hearing and remembering things. Oh right, and I'm also having memory issues. I still haven't processed the switch from paper maps to Waze; I have to reach your friend's house in time to take you to do something extremely important that I can't even remember now (your nails?), and I'm sure I've committed several driving offenses along the way—maybe everything except cattle rustling—since I'm holding a rosary in one hand and a protein bar in the other. On top of that, I can't text while driving, but for my children, making an actual phone call is obsolete. When I ask, "Why don't you just call?" they look at me like I suggested sending a mounted courier, complete with a parchment scroll.

The tragic thing is that by the time I manage to come up with a good answer for my friend who doesn't know why she should remain married, a specimen of some unknown species will have climbed into my car: the female teenager—who, yes, will put on headphones, yet will somehow manage to hear only what she's not supposed to. (I suspect they're the latest model of AirPods, which block sermons, inquiries about grades, and educational proposals, but let every last one of my friends' secrets slip through.)

I only have a few minutes, then, before she gets in and I try to greet her affectionately with, "You smell like Kinder chocolate," at which point she'll recoil and say, "Dark chocolate, thank you—I'm a grown woman now." I only have a few minutes, as I was saying, and I don't even know where to begin: I could write a book to answer my friend's question about why it's always worth staying married. (As a matter of fact, I decided to do exactly that—here it is, you're reading it.) But in the meantime, I call her. When she spirals into the depths, working up a rage like a hamster spinning on its wheel, I'm the only being she has to defend her marriage from every attack. (Aside from Nutella, that is.) All her other friends badmouth her husband, always tell her she's right, or at best advise her to just put up with him. Many of those who have stayed married have built parallel lives under the same roof, try-ing to bother each other as little as possible, yet they're no longer united; there's no real sense of communion between them.

So it's up to me to defend my exhausted friend, as other friends defend me. First, I have to fend off the attacks coming from inside her: the objective fatigue of having turned a very fine but heavy millstone for over twenty years; the bit of loneliness that family life can bring (it's not always easy to socialize and nurture deep relationships when you collapse into bed at night half-dead); plus the fact that her husband, whenever he can, sets himself to "power-saving mode" (he insists it's a way to recharge his testosterone, but it looks suspiciously like a couch to her). And then there are conversations that turn into minefields where they risk fighting over the exact same issue every time (failing to invite his mom over for dinner, the house she chose that ended up being a mistake, as is everything else she does). We won't even mention the near-vertical climb of raising teenage children — and if you have two teenage daughters, both seventeen, the law should allow for advanced technological instruments to be used for pedagogical purposes (like a club).

Then there are the external attacks: the predictable colleague-friend-acquaintance who is so "supportive," her family of origin, and the friends who badmouth her husband or mock him — something we women excel at but which can have toxic consequences. Maybe not glaringly obvious ones, but they run deep.

In short, marriage is a battle, and I'm in charge of reminding my friend it's worth fighting.

But the question she's asking in that message is: *Why?* My husband would say he stays with me because it would be too much trouble learning someone else's name. It really would be a hassle to start from scratch with another wife's likes and dislikes, to figure out survival strategies ... basically, to survive. It seems that avoiding extra effort in relationships might be the North Star for men (with the exception of you, heroic man reading a book about marriage — maybe under duress, but still: you're a male specimen with some optional features, and we salute you).

I, however, want to give my friend a real reason. First of all, I'd remind her that there are children involved — flesh-and-blood combinations of both parents, indivisible because every cell of their bodies is part father, part mother. If they're dragged through a split, they'll get torn apart, and there's no magic fix to glue them back together again afterward. Sure, you can stitch them up, but the scar will remain forever. But more than that, I want to tell her that every marriage is at once a mistake and a miracle. It's a mistake because men and women are the most different, mismatched creatures on Earth (and one day, someone really should ask God about this odd design). Yet it's also a miracle when the two become one. It can happen; I've seen it, I swear.

And even when you don't quite become one—and some marriages struggle mightily, uniting only through great effort and very slowly—marriage is still our one-of-a-kind, irreplaceable opportunity for transformation. And transformation happens only through the Cross; there is no other way. Marriage saves us and helps us let the new self emerge while the old self dies away.

The heart of the matter isn't trying to be perfect or forcing your willpower; it's realizing that the goal is to become the image of God, and the family is the one place where you can truly experience the transforming power of the Cross. Of course, I know all sorts of things might be driving you insane right now—in the meantime, I really have called my friend, and my GPS is telling me I've got seven minutes before the blonde, mysterious entity bursts into my car. Yes, all your criticisms are valid, absolutely on point—and yes, I know that for you, as for me, "You're right" are the sweetest words in the world (they even beat "I love you," and they only tie with "You've lost weight"), so here you go: you're right.

But your issue isn't that two weeks ago your husband refused to go to the dinner that mattered to you so much, and then last night, with a whopping fifteen minutes' notice, came home with a colleague—obviously giving you about six minutes to jam random objects into closets and drawers, assemble something vaguely acceptable, and set an extra place at the table. (And I know that at that moment, you thought about setting two places, one for a Turkish secret-service torturer.) Your problem isn't the idiotic things other people do, or that your husband can't seem to understand you or show kindness or maintain order or whatever else you want him to do; the real problem is our reaction to other people's idiotic behavior. We ourselves are the real problem—our selfishness, our self-centeredness.

We become like Jesus when we carry the Cross among people who weigh heavily on us. And family is the very place for that to happen because in every other relationship, you get to set boundaries; you can say goodbye and walk away. At home, though, you share everything, the masks come off, and living so close together throws your faults right in your face. That's the only time a miracle can occur.

But a crucial step is this: you have to stop obeying yourself and start letting God's Word replace the mad swirl of thoughts erupting in your head, day in and day out. "Turn the other cheek" applies *at home*, not just with the guy who steps on your foot on the bus. If, in a disagreement, you decide to win, by all means go for it—you'll likely succeed, because you're a woman—but then you've fallen into the enemy's logic. If instead you turn the other cheek, you grant another chance, you break the cycle of fighting, and the other person softens.

I personally manage that about once every twenty-six or twenty-seven times I promise myself I'll do it, and only if I deploy distraction tactics—like going for a run, reading a can't-miss article about Rachel McAdams's latest haircut, watching a short video of the 800-meter final, or filling my mouth with something that tastes better than victory, like Venchi's Chocoviar.[1] Never step into the other person's logic in a conflict; if he hurls a stone at you, pick it up and ask, "Did you drop this?" Sometimes you really *are* doing everything for everyone else without anyone noticing, but "if someone takes your cloak, let them have your tunic as well," even if deep down you'd like to snatch it back and give him a smack. In other words, replace your personal script with the Word: "Forgive seventy times seven." Listen to *that*, not to the enemy's voice insisting you're being played, painting your husband in the worst possible light, dredging up his entire history in the words of the accuser ("He's like that because his mother ..." or "He's nicer to that colleague" or "He doesn't care enough," etc.). These accusing thoughts roll along in your mind like desert tumbleweeds.

Stop the gears, go off somewhere alone, don't let anyone see you, and pray. Do it gradually; be patient with yourself, your husband, and your kids. Imagine there's an aquarium full of fish between you and your feelings: you see them there, but you don't listen to them; you don't let them take control.

Little by little, it happens: when you suffer without rebelling, the prince of this world is cast out. And so you're transformed. It's no longer just a marriage—it's a miracle.

Anyway, I'll have to call you back, because I know it's never enough for someone to tell us all this only once. We need a kind of brain-cleansing to counter all the trash our resentful subconscious is constantly spewing. I'll call you back because we all need people around us who help us keep our gaze fixed where it should be, who help us steer our hearts onto a good path and remain grateful for our stories. I'll call you back because my daughter has now gotten into the car and, as a grand gesture of respect for me, decided to

---

[1] Italian chocolates.

blast her music through the car speakers instead of just burying herself in her headphones. She's cranking out some tune at a million decibels. I'm not complaining, because if I say, "Can you turn it down?" that's high treason and would be punished with silence, a disgusted scowl, and an enormous eye roll, all of which essentially convey unmentionable thoughts about me. (One of the few rules I've managed to uphold at home is "no swearing"; the strongest outburst allowed is "*che palle*.")[2]

So here I am, maintaining an air of calm at about ninety-seven decibels of something I don't recognize.

"Do you like *uno Marzo?*"[3]

"Sure, I like the first, the second, the third ... March is a great month."

"I asked if you like Bruno Mars."

It's official. I'm deaf.

---

[2] *Che palle* is Italian slang used to express annoyance; "what a pain in the butt!"
[3] The author hears her daughter say *uno Marzo*, which means "March 1."

Chapter One

Why Stay Married Even if ...

We Don't Love Each Other Anymore

Going to dinner at Silvia and Giovanni's can be a bit of a blow to my self-esteem. They're a well-oiled team, and when they have guests over, they look like a Formula 1 pit crew: you're still standing there with your jacket on, solemnly admiring the flawless table setting, and they've already timed the pasta to perfection so that it's ready right at the moment when the last bacon-wrapped prune is snatched off the appetizer platter. Meanwhile, two children, wearing white shirts and with hair evenly combed, are quietly seated on the couch with a book. And that's when I start wondering where I went wrong.

Because, at best, I might manage to set the table and serve a meal that's only slightly burned on roughly the agreed-upon evening (or possibly at dawn the next day), but there's always a choice to be made: either dinner or kids dressed nicely. (And definitely never in white shirts, which are reserved for only the most solemn occasions, like Confirmations or the Confederations Cup final.) As for sitting politely on the couch, my kids would have liked to, but unfortunately they were usually busy with high-stakes military operations—like torturing a younger sibling who was hog-tied after winning a round of PlayStation. I speak in the past tense because now they're adults and can even manage to put on a shirt without my help—an item they tend to abandon on the floor, only to rediscover it clean in their closet through a process they only vaguely understand (like photosynthesis). But aside from that, they're not much help when I have guests, because manual dexterity isn't their strong suit. ("Berni, can you help me wrap this bowl with plastic film?" "Sure, you hold it still, I'll rotate the entire kitchen.")

This is why I find it so hard to believe that Silvia and Gio's wonderful, slick, war-machine routine could ever jam. Yet a few nights ago, after dinner, I nearly had a heart attack. I followed Silvia into the kitchen while she was clearing the dishes—which normally I'd never do, because I belong to the school of thought that says you should never enter another woman's kitchen right after dinner. (You might see things you're better off not seeing—like hygiene practices straight out of some Calcutta street-food stand.) But I inevitably wind up clearing at least a fork, just so I look like a decent person.

Anyway, when I followed her in with my single dutiful fork, Silvia looked at me and said, "I don't love him anymore." Just like that, out of nowhere, casually and coolly.

At first, I wasn't too startled, because my friend sometimes experiences what we call her "universal-judgment meltdown"—that "I've messed up everything, my life is a disaster" moment. I know all I need to do is listen and let her vent. Maybe her son got in trouble at school, or she got told off at work, or her husband gave her a snappy answer, and that sets off fifteen minutes of crisis. I know she'll say the worst things about herself, her husband, and their entire story, looking back on it with a harsh, critical eye. She's actually right, of course—yes, she's right—but if we start from a place of "I've been wronged," the numbers never add up. And I know this for a fact, because "I'm Right" is basically my middle name. That's exactly how the accuser works: he keeps whispering words of judgment and negativity, hiding all the good we have, showing us only the flaws and the weariness.

So I let Silvia talk, and then I patiently start tearing her accusations down. One of the main tasks of a friend, after all, is to bless our life when we can't see it with the right eyes—to remind us that it's good, that *we* are good, that everything happening to us is good, that God does everything well. Sometimes we need someone else to help us remember that. Ever since Eden, the same old temptation keeps popping up: "God is out to get you." That's why it's crucial to keep watch over our hearts and, if possible, over the hearts of those who ask us (or allow us) to do so. It's like defending a territory—staying fully present, patrolling every inch, watching out for words, feelings, thoughts, and temptations. The hardest work we're asked to do is to keep our eyes fixed on Heaven. Because the very moment we take our gaze off God and put it on our own grievances, we fall—like when you're riding a bike and start staring at your feet. And that changes everything about our suffering.

In fact, when someone asks, "How's it going?" our knee-jerk reaction is usually to complain a bit; we don't spontaneously answer that we're happy simply to have ears that can hear the question. Which, by the way, means we already have plenty to be happy about: we're alive, we can hear, we can talk, we'll probably have lunch and dinner soon, and there's a good chance we have a bed to sleep in and breakfast the next day. For the sake of accuracy, I should admit that this "Pollyanna mode"—as my kids call it—makes them want to throttle that bony little girl who takes possession of me at these moments. It doesn't help them appreciate life's wonders at all—especially if they're flipping out because DAZN[4] isn't working during the big match and they're

---

[4] A sports streaming service.

Blessed Is the Day We "Got It Wrong"

about to miss a free kick. In times like those, if I told them not to be upset because at least we have a couch and a TV, they'd probably beat me up. As for my daughters, they consider complaining a constitutional right, on par with using eyelash curlers, so: "Pollyanna, get lost."

Anyway, I assumed Silvia's dramatic declaration was just one of those off-the-cuff, seemingly harmless gripes—like venting because you have a friend at hand, so why not take advantage? And sure, blowing off steam can feel therapeutic, but sometimes it only feeds our discontent. You're basically okay, but you start casually listing the ways your life isn't perfect, or criticizing someone, and the negativity starts to rise and swell. Complaining provides fuel for the subconscious (one way of referring to Satan), who thrives on our sulking, our so-called "insights," and especially on the idea that "I should always say what I feel." So we do need to be careful when venting: in small doses, for occasional personal use—keeping in mind it can become addictive. Words change the climate of the heart: they stoke our feelings, letting us drift along with the current. If we want to stay anchored to the rock of our true good, the only thing we can oppose to all this chatter, to the emotional outburst, is God's Word. We need something objective to hold onto, something solid. Sometimes, for me, what makes me pass judgment on my own life are genuine, serious issues that require work and prayer. Other times, they're just silly triggers—and for most of us non–Gisele Bündchen types, all it takes is opening social media to feel like a walrus. One minute I'm reading a meditation by St. Anselm, feeling almost mystically inclined, and the next I'm zooming in on a photo of that Brazilian supermodel's butt.

In short, my heart swings between the *Summa Theologiae* and *Vogue*, which is a sure sign it's totally unreliable. Indeed, only

God can convert and heal us with prevenient grace, but *we* still have a role to play: our willingness. To resist "where your heart wants to take you," we have to replace our unconscious (and our odd self-made religion) with the Word of God, which really tells us who God is and provides the only objective measure of reality—anchoring our hearts to the capital-T Truth.

So going back to Silvia, I initially thought her mini-crisis was just a torrent of words I needed to hear out and contain. But then I saw a new resolve in her eyes: "Forget becoming one flesh—I'd rather kill him in his sleep." Now, I'll admit there can be moments in a marriage when loving feelings fall off a cliff—like today, when my husband shattered an expensive Vietri ceramic plate, and my distress ("We don't have a single intact twelve-piece set!") was met with, "They're ugly anyway; I didn't even want to buy 'em. They look like some preschool clay project"; or when he asks what he should give me for my birthday since I "don't need anything" (as if "need" has anything to do with it—I have a leather-bound wish list in multiple volumes!)—but no, killing him in his sleep never occurred to me. How would I manage on my own? I have no idea how to pump gas, pay the car tax, change a tire, squash a cockroach, understand what's happening in the Middle East, or breathe calmly when the kids come home late. We've basically split our lives in half: I have certain tasks, he has others (and I make it sound more like a corporate workflow chart than a romantic statement—I don't say I love him because he hates that kind of sentimentality; let's just say I have a favorable opinion of him).

"All I know," Silvia continues, "is that when we got married, he didn't know how to do anything around the house, and it didn't bother me. Now he's like Furio." (For those of you who aren't old Italians like me, Furio is a character from a Carlo Verdone movie.)[5] "He nags if I use degreaser on wood or buy fruit out of season. Like I'd know which fruit is in season? For me, it's only 'out of season' if I get to the supermarket after eight and the store's closed. I want my original base-model man back. When he lived with his college roommate, the only fruit he ever consumed was the strawberry in his Daiquiri, and his idea of keeping the apartment clean was opening a window when the room was too smoky and throwing out pizza boxes when they blocked the door. Back then, his weekly portion of veggies was the basil on his mozzarella. Now he steams me up some *malva* leaves!" (Which, for me, is just a Chanel nail polish color—shade 137, to be precise.)

I try to piece together what's changed. Silvia explains that he's had some issues at work—an important career slowdown. Like many men who are no longer at the starting line and no longer pumped up with the energy of younger colleagues, he's withdrawn a bit. In his disillusionment, it's as if he gave up on the professional side of his life, losing all drive. He's basically pre-retiring. Financially, they're in a comfortable spot—investments from the glory days—and with the kids growing up, he's turned his focus more toward family and home, pulling in the oars. He's become a couch fixture, rarely wants to go out, and no longer exercises. The lean guy in a Burberry suit she married is still there, presumably, but he's now buried inside someone wearing a tracksuit twice his size.

"Look, Silvia," I tell her, "it's still better to have him on the couch than to have a fifty-something who's suddenly obsessed with amino acids, signs up for mindfulness training, runs sprints in the stadium wearing compression socks, or flips out over his hotshot accountant padel partner."

---

[5] Furio is an obsessive and neurotic character.

"Yeah, but now it's like he has no idea who he is or what role he plays, whether at home or out in the world," Silvia replies. She reminds me how, for years, he was basically excluded from a huge part of the mother-child dynamic—like many fathers who were never initiated into the arcane art of assembling a school-supply kit. (Sometimes, at the start of September, the brand of watercolor pencils the teacher insists on can only be found on the black market: they vanish from stationery stores, and you have to get in good with the Magliana gang.[6] (Not to mention that's still less terrifying than a parents' chat group, where you're forced to join waves of mandatory outrage—like Fridays for Future and SeNonOraQuando—or be branded a pariah.)[7]

For years, Giovanni traveled constantly for work—one week in New York, the next in Tokyo—so Silvia handled everything on her own. Suddenly, as circumstances changed, he was there with her in all these situations she'd always faced alone. "Good grief, woman, do you realize how many headaches you're spared now?" I ask her. Some people, after a single thread about picking out a teacher's gift, are ready to sell their children to organ dealers and buy a house in Nepal. Having someone to share the domestic load is a huge relief, though learning to actually *do* things as a couple isn't easy—hence why many couples end up leading parallel lives, sharing almost nothing. The artisan work of doing life together as a couple requires patience and dedication.

Meanwhile, when the kids arrived, Silvia had devoted herself to-tally to them, as so many women do—since we're basically designed

---

[6] The Banda della Magliana was a far-right Italian criminal organization in Rome.

[7] Respectively, Fridays for Future and SeNonOraQuando are en-
vironmentalist and feminist protest movements popular in Italy.

to nurture life, or at least help it along in its most vulnerable state. Maybe our risk, then, is turning children into idols, building exclusive relationships with them that leave Dad on the outside, cut off. During their early years of marriage, while Giovanni was rocketing up in his career, Silvia—keeping her own job on a minimal schedule—became a full-on competitive mom. She was the kind who'd grab the front-row seat at the kids' show, camera in hand and a bouquet of flowers ready to honor her daughter's brilliant performance as the piece of tumbleweed. (Meanwhile, my kids were usually given donkey ears that actually looked more like a rabbit's, plus a guaranteed case of head lice. "I'll ask the teacheu if duwing the play I can have a scwatch," my youngest once told me.) Silvia is one of those mothers who read every page of the school's mission statement and raised children who ask for Swiss chard at dinner. These mothers don't count green candy as a source of vitamins. They sign their kids up for violin lessons, and by high school, they're already having them read Greek historians in the original (albeit with a parallel translation, thank goodness).

During those years, Silvia unknowingly dug a moat that cut her off from her husband, as often happens. The kids fulfilled her, and there was no more shared daily life or genuine closeness. Occasionally, when she needed him, she'd rattle his cage by going a little crazy.

(A quick note for any male readers: when we women go crazy, it's because we want to be loved. I realize "to want" and "to be loved" don't go nicely together in one sentence, but the underlying message is: "Feel free to love me—but if you don't, you'll pay." Of course, we want men to love us spontaneously, but in exactly the way we demand. Respecting a man's freedom is tough. The opposite of love isn't hate; it's possessiveness, trying to control the other person's freedom—a trap that lies in wait for men and women alike.)

(A quick note for women: when we stop trying to control a man or measure everything he does or doesn't do for us, and instead focus on *being lovable*, that's when he'll do the things that please us. Not because he likes them, but (if he's a decent guy) because he wants his woman to be happy. If we manage to remove that sense of expectation from our looks and our words, we'll get from him all that we desire.)

But the first thing Silvia needs to hear in response to "I don't love him anymore" is that the notion of effortless romantic love is just that—a notion. When you *feel* love, sooner or later it fades or disappoints, runs dry. That's why, as Denis de Rougemont explains in *Love in the Western World*, we invented the idea of "impossible love," which feels infinite thanks to some obstacle in the way. Once the obstacle is gone, the supposedly "romantic" love vanishes as well.

Love isn't a feeling—or not just that, not always. Love is (also) a decision, a choice, a path, a mission—one that can be complicated by all sorts of factors beyond our control, like personal hang-ups, childhood wounds, or family background. Still, our eternal life hinges on that mission. If, as St. John of the Cross says, we'll be judged at the end of our lives by how well we have loved, then for us married folk, that love for our spouse will come before the love for those "famished African children" who were such persistent imaginary dinner guests in our kids' childhood. ("Eat your dinner, or the kids in Africa …")

And staking everything on love for just one person, with all its risks, shadows, and hidden corners, is a huge gamble—a total risk, an all-in in poker terms. The problem with Christianity today is that it's basically merged with bourgeois society, the kind born out of the French Revolution, where the individual rarely has to take any real risk (and, not coincidentally, divorce was introduced pretty early on). Yet we know that in marriage, we really do wager our eternal life.

Blessed Is the Day We "Got It Wrong"

Of course, this isn't the time to give Silvia a sermon on eternal life, because there are moments when preaching simply won't help. If I were a man and so were she—two buddies talking—this might be the time for a good punch in the face. In fact, I know a man, a faithful guy with plenty of biceps, who did exactly that to his best friend upon learning he'd cheated on his wife. He pulled him aside and said, "Drop your mistress, and I'll pretend I didn't hear a thing." When his friend hesitated, he punched him in the face a couple of times. Unbelievably, it worked. The blows must have snapped him out of his trance. Sometimes an outsider, a friend, can see your life more clearly than you do, especially the mess you're about to wade into. Of course, you have to want to listen. Many people would rather listen to the stand-in for love they think they've found in an affair, or cling to their anger, resentment, or even just the end—or rather, the transformation—of the feeling they had at the start of dating or marriage.

But feeling is only one element in building a love story, and it's not always the one we should heed. It's like the spark that lights the fuse, the foam atop the wave, while the long flow of the river that runs from spring to sea—our life—is a much lengthier journey. Sometimes you're underwater and just need to hang on until you can resurface without thrashing around too much; other times, you catch the wave and glide gracefully like a seasoned surfer. We stay together for reasons different from those that initially brought us together. Love changes as we do. Silvia can learn to love this new version of Giovanni.

Sometimes there are *Big Wednesday*[8] moments with the perfect wave, and other times there are long stretches of waiting where the water's barely rippling. I know many men and women who were

---

[8]   A 1978 film about surfers.

able to *not* listen to their feelings during those rough patches, when they had to reinvent their marriage—moments when "listening to your heart" was not an option; you just had to push on, head down, to stay afloat. In fact, everyone I know who has remained married has had to do it at some point or another.

Among these people is my friend whose wife attempted suicide, or my friend who was betrayed by her husband. They found a way to love against the grain, stubbornly, going against their own gut reactions. They knew how to love *for two* and for long stretches, driven not by a spontaneous feeling but by deliberate resolve. Even when a marriage doesn't demand some heroic act, a certain heroism is needed—doled out regularly—during challenging phases, like the teenage years of your kids. Teens are experts at wedging themselves into every crack between their parents to trigger fights. Living with a teenager (or maybe I should say "teenage daughter," because that's a whole different thing than the male version) can feel like a round of Russian roulette: you never know if your words will fire a fatal shot. You just stand still with your eyes shut, waiting. The best outcome is coming out alive; in other words, if you're lucky, your daughter won't kill you this time, but no matter what you say, she'll roll her eyes in despair at having such a clueless mother.

Thinking about the couples I know, it's obvious each one has had to reinvent themselves, sometimes multiple times: changes in finances, life circumstances, jobs, dealing with illness or a child's disability, the empty nest, over-involved or absent or dysfunctional families of origin, relatives needing care, inheritance disputes, blowups, personal crises—you name it. Every couple has its share of struggles, though for some marriages, it's clearly heavier than for others.

What makes the difference is knowing we're not alone in this battle. If we fight to stay together, God fights with us, because the

Blessed Is the Day We "Got It Wrong"

sacrament has made that union sacred. Unfortunately, God tends to act slowly, like rain or snow—no magic wand. He changes things gradually and, truth be told, sometimes doesn't change them at all. Sometimes He won't remove our martyrdom: we want relief, but He wants humility. He leaves us certain sufferings because He wants us leaning on Him in our frailty—that emptiness, that longing. If nothing were missing in our lives, we wouldn't be precarious—and maybe we wouldn't even think of praying. (By the way, "precarious" and "prayer" share the same Latin root.)

That supposedly "wrong" story of yours is there for a reason. It keeps you clinging to Christ: if you understand that, you've hit the jackpot. And that's the most valuable thing to say when a marriage gets tough: bless your struggle, your trial, the pain you're experiencing, because it's your path for being joined to God. It's the only path you were given—only those circumstances, that story, can be the right context for meeting Him. And only *you* can understand that in the context of your own life.

I hope Silvia takes that step and embraces this new chapter. It seems hard to reverse the direction her husband has chosen—pushing him back into his old professional life might be a lost cause. It's more important for Silvia to revisit some basic rules (which, honestly, I need to hear for myself, too, every so often). Rule number one: stop trying to change your husband. Your spouse is your path to God. How can a blind person guide another blind person? If your husband is going through a difficult transition and is a bit stuck, remember: when someone in the couple is depressed or caught in the middle of a tough, existential turning point, you don't follow them into their private Hell. (See C. S. Lewis's *The Great Divorce*, in which one partner tries to drag the other into his Hell, but the other refuses to go.) You need a good, faithful core inside you and a protective layer of Band-Aids all around, accepting that the other person might hurt you.

Second rule: if women tend to be sensitive to affection, men are sensitive to respect. We weigh these things differently. When you don't value what your husband does—when you always contradict him or never consider his ideas—you might think lightly of it because you still love him even if you disagree. But remember, it hurts him the way you feel hurt if you sense you're not loved. (Could someone please tattoo that on my forehead? Because I always forget.)

If the failure—the only true failure of our life—is not to love, then we should apply ourselves to the care of love with the devotion of a monk. Just as a monk respects silence, prays at set times, and works in the monastery, we should be equally conscientious about avoiding the baggy underwear with the torn elastic, thermal pajamas, no makeup, visible roots, and frumpy "house clothes" worn under the pretext of "Who's going to see me anyway?" We need to carve out couple time, make ourselves apologize, and get creative in doing nice things for each other—even when the other person seems determined to be as unpleasant as possible. We have to break free from the routine of the same old phrases and gestures and come up with something to remind both ourselves and our spouse that this relationship matters more than anything else.

The real problem is that each of us has a spark of Lucifer-like spirit that just *has* to have the last word. But we have to switch off Radio Satan. One day, I literally bit the inside of my cheek until it bled just to stop myself from saying "I told you so." Naturally, I remember it well because that only happens about once every thirteen or fourteen years; usually, I not only say "I told you so," I get it embroidered in gold thread on a lovely floral tapestry with letters a meter high.

Blessed Is the Day We "Got It Wrong"

And then there's the issue of waiting versus demanding: we women—scarred by Original Sin and sometimes by our personal sins—can become bottomless pits of the urge to control. The real question is how we respond to that internal demand, or, rather, *who* we ask to respond to it.

So, Silvia, all I can say is take your eyes off your husband and fix them on the only One who can fill that bottomless void. Instead of calling a friend, grab your rosary; instead of scrolling aimlessly through social media, go sit before the tabernacle—or, if you can't, pick up a rosary like a weapon and open fire. Do whatever you can, as best you can, to love him right where he is in this difficult stretch. We have no power to generate change in anyone. The only thing we can change is our own gaze, our own heart—which, as the psalm says, is an abyss, and healing it is no small feat. All we can do is guard it—watchful, attentive, trying to be our best selves.

What I can promise you, from all the listening I've done, is that this season of struggle will pass. But I'm not saying that to encourage settling for less; I'm talking about the *something more* hiding beneath the surface. I promise there will be a day when you look at a breathtaking view—or maybe just admire your own nicely toned quad, or the tidied spice drawer in the kitchen (everyone's heart is stirred by something different)—and you'll wonder how you ever doubted your love for this man who's so perfect for you. Or at least, made perfect for the story of *your* salvation by the sacrament of marriage.

Chapter Two

Why Stay Married Even if ...

Things Aren't Working in Bed Anymore

"**C**ostanza, you're always disparaging frumpy clothes and granny underwear. You're the apostle of lacy lingerie and mandatory makeup. Please, say something to my wife: she doesn't desire me anymore. She doesn't come after me. She doesn't take care of herself. Or rather, she only does so for the outside world, but when it's my turn, she whips out the over-sized sack-pajamas. It's been so long since I've had any action that pretty soon the World Wildlife Fund will classify me as a protected species. So tell me, is it really so abnormal if my mind goes wandering when a woman whose breasts are bigger than an A-cup smiles at me?"

I'm going to stop you right there, buddy who's confiding in me like we're bros (maybe because I don't even have an A-cup, more like an inverted version). I appreciate your honesty and frank friendship, but just so we don't end up swapping belches on the couch, let me make it clear: I'm on Team Wives. We women have a sort of intraspecies solidarity—we know things you men would never understand—so I'm not going to join in criticizing her for messy ponytails improvised with a pencil, for being a few pounds overweight, for going makeup-free and rocking that classic "fog in the Po Valley" complexion.[9] She's probably eating lunch at the vending machine on the second floor, snacking while her groceries sit in the supermarket cart, then eating dinner in three separate waves — first while cooking, then sitting at the table, and then again while clearing up, in that endless slog toward the bed. Of course I instinctively take your wife's side. But then, when you're not listening, I'll tell her she'd better not push her luck too far.

Sex isn't everything, but it does matter, and I've seen more than one marriage end — or come close to it — for testosterone (or estrogen) reasons. Sometimes couples let things go, forgetting to nurture that intimacy which can be a soothing oasis along what can sometimes feel like a desert path. This shared space is the height of your communion, so guard it with joy.

But let me add something, friend who's devoured all my books and imagines me prowling around at home like a panther, wearing feather-tipped high-heeled slippers, a silk robe, and fluttery lashes. Sure, it would be amazing if I actually did all the things I tell others to do (a piece of advice is basically a good example that never quite made it). In reality, I often forget that I'm a wife who needs to seduce her husband every day. I default to "I'm beautiful on the inside" mode (I mean, who's going to flip me inside out to check?), and sometimes I throw on stuff from my junior-high years — so old it's now ironically avant-garde. A few years ago, I blamed my lack of style on the fact that my kids were little and my entire beauty routine was basically brushing my teeth, finding a

---

9 The Po Valley in northern Italy is often blanketed in fog, so a "fog in the Po Valley complexion" refers to a pale or subdued appearance caused by a lack of sunlight, especially in someone who would normally be tan otherwise.

t-shirt without spit-up stains, and applying mascara at traffic lights. Now that they're older, my downfall comes from aging: it takes more and more time simply to maintain a baseline of aesthetic dignity—cover-lift-smooth-moisturize-color-tone—just so I don't frighten small children on the street. I suspect there was a golden moment of peak beauty for me somewhere in the middle, lasting perhaps fifteen minutes—during which I was probably asleep or stuck at a condo association meeting.

I mean, sure, I believe Jennifer Lopez can do an Intimissimi[10] commercial even over age fifty, get married five times (twice to that gorgeous hunk Ben Affleck), and then write into the marriage contract that they'll have sex four times a week. On top of being naturally gorgeous, she has an entire team to keep her that way: aestheticians, a personal nail artist (apparently "quartz effect" is in this year, rather than chipped polish from the department store clearance rack), and of course a hairdresser—unlike us subhumans, who can barely achieve the distinguished "home-caregiver" shade skillfully created by mixing grown-out roots with highlights that are way past due.

Right—almost forgot a disclaimer: I wanted to say this chapter is off-limits to minors, but I can't help feeling sad about that, because a lot of minors already know and have seen way more than I do about sexuality. So let me just offer a warning: I've heard many stories of people's intimate lives, but this topic is so delicate, so personal and private, that for once I don't feel up to handing out a "how-to" guide. I know, it's incredible—normally, the moment I grasp even a tiny part of something, I start dishing out advice: if I so much as figure out which side is supposed to score in soccer, I think I'm the national team coach; if I don't

---

[10] An Italian lingerie brand.

burn the ragù, I'm writing a cookbook. But here, I'll just share a few modest insights I've stumbled across in my own experience and in that of many friends.

With that said, let me try to answer you, dear friend with a wife who's gotten sloppy and forgotten how to seduce you.

Some of us (a lot of us?) lead lives that, in my opinion, can be called heroic. Busy, sure, but heroic. And I don't say that in a whining tone. Actually, my kids say I'm "randomly happy," so let's be clear: I'm grateful for everything I have. Whenever it's cold out, I get a thrill stepping back into my house, and it even surprises me a bit that I managed to buy one (well, three-quarters of it—the rest belongs to the bank, but so far none of them have shown up asking to sleep over). I'm grateful to be alive, to be baptized, to know lots of people (some even sane); I'm grateful for a million things I won't list now. Random sampling: my family, A.G.E. Interrupter by SkinCeuticals (a gift), my love of running (plus having two working feet to do it with), the YSL purse I own (also a gift, like everything I have that's of any real value). I'm grateful for each circumstance in my life, and even for what's missing, because I know this specific story—precisely this one—is where I'll meet God. Here I am, face-to-face with the emptiness that worries me, angers me, and challenges me, and the fullness that makes me happy and satisfies me. Sometimes staying in that gratitude is tough—though my experiences (and many encounters) make it obvious there are plenty of lives much harder than mine, and some that are much easier.

We all fight to remain faithful to our daily routines, and it can be a heavy, heroic lift to do things properly: stooping to pick up a pencil, sewing a button back on rather than leaving it undone, changing the water in a vase of flowers before they start to stink, showing up on time for the merciless dental hygienist (even if the last person who found a parking spot near the office had to buy a bicycle just so he wouldn't lose that space). Nothing tragic, sure, but sometimes cleaning up the kitchen can feel daunting when all you want is to curl up inside a giant vat of Nutella. And so we push on, honoring daily schedules and responsibilities (including children we must pick up at two in the morning), enduring the torments inflicted by teenage daughters trained by North Korean intelligence to keep you perpetually anxious—often with just enough money, but never loads (apparently God loves a good thrill and wants to keep us praying). If I die, I'll leave all my lactic acid to my friends, as my son announced at age eight when he took off for his "secret mission" in Afghanistan.

Amidst all this, my friend, it isn't always easy to stay lighthearted and keep up your energy in the bedroom—collapsing into bed after a twenty-hour day, barely remembering the name of the man lying next to you. It's hard to maintain any romantic spark when the day's been one long chain of chores and hand-offs between spouses, when you can't find ten minutes for a real conversation (the grocery list doesn't count—and anyway, my husband's monthly total for meaningful dialogue is ten minutes), or downtime to recall that everything you once chose each other for is still there and has probably grown. You need a conscious decision.

And here's where I trot out the usual clichés—yes, clichés from women's magazines, but they're true: it's vital—truly vital, not just important—to plan exclusive time together, even when it's the last thing you want because, of the last forty-eight hours you spent together, forty-seven were used to argue about the heating or the laundry rack in the living room. Even just looking each other in the face for reasons unrelated to recovering the SPID[11]

---

[11] Italy's digital identification system.

password or deciding who's picking up the lab results can be precious. Carving out a bit of time for just the two of you is as necessary as grocery shopping. It's something you must schedule without compromise and without guilt toward anyone else, even when things are good. If things aren't working physically, you might try recreating what worked in the past—maybe going out to dinner, taking a trip, strolling hand in hand—fiercely protecting and nurturing that time and space for the couple. The big problem here is that the crisis remains manageable only until some outside disturbance shows up—like a coworker or acquaintance who says, "It's just a drink, we're only friends, what's the harm?" If there's already a break in the intimacy at home, it's harder to keep things on course.

Sexuality is a language, and we have to practice speaking it, especially as freshness fades and we need to reach a deeper level. There's no magic formula. A sexual relationship is built through everyday thoughtfulness—actually showing you're trying to love each other, with both words and gestures. Karol Wojtyła gave us a bold and beautiful perspective on sexuality—first as a bishop, working with engaged couples, in his wonderful *Love and Responsibility*, and later as pope in his teachings on the Theology of the Body: *Man and Woman He Created Them*. This teaching is nothing like the prudish or uptight stereotypes about Christianity. Sexuality isn't something to worship or fear or despise; it's a precious gift from God to a man and a woman. But like everything else—"Nothing in man is without fault if it lacks Your strength"—it needs healing. It's God's love that heals our sexuality, making it good for spouses—turning it into an essential part of the couple's path toward perfection, because in the difference between man and woman, we find the road to holiness, to fulfillment. This is completely the opposite of those jokes that go, "According to the

Church, if you're not married, you can't have sex. And if you are married, you can, but only grudgingly."

In reality, the Church is the number-one fan of genuine intimacy between man and woman. This is massive news, if you think about it: you don't become holy *in spite of* the body but *through* the body. It's not some dirty thing to be mortified; it's a vehicle of sanctification. Far from being sex-phobic, the Church has the guts to say that spouses, with mutual listening, love, and acceptance—with patient timing and respect for each other's dignity—can become saints *through* their physical union. The heart of the matter is the person as a whole—a body, a soul, and a spirit—all meant to become one with the other. The body cannot be overlooked. But it's never just *a* body: it's *that* particular body, with its history and its soul.

That's precisely why the rampant pornography that's so easily accessible to everyone—of any age—is the polar opposite of real sexuality. Porn is all about bodies—actually, it's about genitals without any person attached—whereas the sexuality God intended is between two people who choose to walk side by side, supporting and welcoming each other, forgiving each other. And in that embrace, the body takes center stage as an instrument of communion. I suspect the damage from widespread porn use is incalculable. I also think anyone caught in that trap needs a path to heal both heart and vision. It can be done, yes, but mainstream culture doesn't see it as necessary. Still, it *is* possible. I'm not saying we can revert to the innocence of my two-year-old daughter who saw a magazine cover featuring a topless woman and asked, "Mommy, why is that lady showing all her milk to everyone?" But we can ask for the grace of a clean gaze.

In all honesty, I used to think porn was only a problem for teenage boys—or maybe even children, sadly—but not for adults.

Then a few days ago, I found out differently when a wife confided that her oh-so-upstanding husband—the kind of guy you'd bet on for impeccable behavior—the father of her children, in fact—uses it compulsively during work trips or up in their attic. Below that seemingly beautiful, harmonious home, with an attractive wife, he's sneaking off for porn. You say to yourself, "Impossible! I refuse to believe a middle-aged man"—(yes, I'm dropping the bomb: at fifty, you're middle-aged, even if you still call each other "guys" at forty plus)—"a father and a successful professional, is doing that." And yet, yes. To keep living this lie, this personal divorce from himself, he's developed a kind of schizophrenia, always split in two. He's never entirely authentic. His wife says she no longer recognizes him. She feels like she doesn't even know who he is. Because no matter what he's doing—at home, outside, at work—he's lying. When you're split like that, you're always split, not just when you're watching porn. He's lying to himself before he lies to his wife and kids—and even worse, to his daughters, who will shape their understanding of men based on their relationship with him.

Honestly, I'm not sure what advice to give her. (In the holy of holies of the marital bed, only the spouses and God belong.) But I've tried to gather some seeds of common sense, so here's what I'd say if we were a bit closer.

First, don't freak out and throw your marriage away. Try to see your husband as a man in a moment of weakness. Rather than giving in to your first impulse (which, for me, would be to clobber him), pray for him. Fast for him, because "there are certain demons that can only be driven out by prayer and fasting," and if a demon isn't at work here, then I don't know where else he'd be. Struggle past your wounded pride and hurt feelings. Right now, he's going through a rough time, but if you two manage to win this battle together, he'll more than make it up to you. (And you can serve some fitting punishment later, maybe a marathon of romantic movies where he's forbidden from stepping out whenever there's a kiss scene, like my husband does when I try to watch them.)

Second, seek help. Turn to another couple who can guide you, a priest, a therapist, someone further along the road. The humiliation of admitting this weakness to your wife is a grueling but necessary step. It's a powerful weapon. And it's crucial for him to have someone to answer to when he's up against temptation or if he slips again. He needs allies—at least one person he can be completely open with in his fight. Maybe that person can't be you, because he might not be able to come to you every time he's tempted. Yet knowing you know—even though it humiliates him—actually helps him heal.

Third, in dealing with the porn problem, ask yourselves what's missing between the two of you, both "by day" and in the bedroom. We have to be honest: if everything had been truly great, this probably wouldn't have happened.

If I can be frank—though I'm not sure I can, not directly—her husband might be Mr. Hyde, but in my view, she's a bit psycho too. Maybe it's because she comes from those Swedish islands where the sun doesn't rise for three months at a stretch. Or maybe, ironically, that same sun is blazing nineteen hours a day in the summer and she's had enough. I see her sometimes at morning Mass (yes, there are Catholics in Sweden, a whopping 1 percent of the population, and the rest look at them the way they looked at Pippi Longstocking when she was lifting her horse, Old Man). She's definitely not Pippi, though: she's sort of chilly and reserved— while I, who'll chat with a fire hydrant, must have struck her as a caveman when we first met. I'm surprised she confided in me at all, since we're not that close. (Maybe she doesn't talk to anyone except call-center reps, and I'm slightly better than Marco from Telecom—or possibly even Luca from Sky.) I don't know—maybe her standoffishness, which once didn't bug her husband, is now tough in the daily grind, especially with all they have to manage.

Still, who really knows? Each of us is a mystery by ourselves; a couple is basically a faraway galaxy with hidden patterns and rules. Obviously, something was off between them, and that's the hardest part: patiently starting over, rebuilding, seeking intimacy with a man whose secret habits have left you repulsed—someone you'd sooner poke with a fork (like roast beef in the oven, just to see what juice seeps out). But as I said, they should carve out time for each other. They need the courage to say what they want from each other. I know a couple who took a "vacation" together not to some Caribbean paradise but right in their own town. They booked a hotel for one night, close enough so the grandparents could call if needed, dressed up for a fancy dinner—no cutesy teddy-bear pajamas. In their case, the marriage was in rough shape. At first they had no idea what to say to each other. But starting with that strange, local getaway, step by step, they began reconnecting with gestures of tenderness and care. Eventually, they remembered what made them choose each other years before that storm.

Another point I want to raise is that spontaneity is overrated in this department. "I don't feel like it" or "It's just not happening" can't always be the final word. If your husband wants to talk, you can't perpetually say you're not in the mood. And by "talk," I mean *that* language, the one men around here typically find more compelling than verbal chit-chat. (Afterward, if I try to say to my husband, "Let's talk," he replies, "Go ahead and start," and falls asleep in less than a second.) Yes, men should make more effort to talk with actual words, but women shouldn't completely refuse to speak the other language. I'm not saying you should always get ready for intimacy with the zeal of a seventeen-year-old heading to a party where she'll see her future husband (though he doesn't know he's her future husband). That's the pinnacle of aesthetic anxiety: "Oh my gosh, look at my tummy" (flat as a board), "I have terrible skin" (taut as a drum). Of course we can relax a bit over time. But self-care still plays an important role: it's part of the attitude that says, "I'm here for you, I take care of myself because I respect you as a man." If any hardcore feminist sees this, she'll probably want me committed, but always being there for the other person—sometimes pushing past a lousy mood or fatigue—is precious. As my friend Fr. Dario likes to say, "If you're not in the mood, get in the mood."

Men also have a role to play. For instance, they need to remember we women don't have an on/off switch, unlike them. You can't spend all day being grouchy or aloof and then expect things to click in bed, as some men do. That's just not how we operate. Everything is interconnected for us. The great Wojtyła, once again, wrote that "most cases of female discomfort, neurosis, or frigidity stem from a woman feeling reduced to an object of pleasure." Once again, the heart of it all is the *person*, seen integrally. For a woman to experience pleasure, he explains, the man must "understand and respect the difference in his own physical and psychological rhythm compared to hers." "He must take into account," he continues in *Love and Responsibility*, "that a woman naturally finds it harder to adapt to a man. This is due to the divergence of their physical and psychic rhythms. Therefore, a 'harmonization' is necessary, which cannot happen without a conscious effort of the will—above all on the part of the man—without carefully observing the woman." You need attentiveness, tenderness. That's how a sexual relationship becomes a genuine, mutual self-gift for spouses, thereby teaching them both what true love is. And it cuts both ways: loving each other leads to a better physical relationship, and having a satisfying physical relationship often helps you love each other more. It can defuse tension, smooth out disagreements, and help the two of you make up after a fight.

Seeing each other as whole persons also means rejecting any method of contraception. When we give our bodies to one another, we receive the other person *entirely*, ready to welcome the consequences. This is what it means to practice natural methods: paying attention to fertile periods and always leaving God the final say over any children He might entrust to us. I know even in Catholic circles nobody really talks about this anymore, let alone outside them, but natural methods do work—partly because they keep desire strong. Either you can't do it all the time (and we all know forbidden fruit is extra-tempting), or, if you ignore the rules, there's added suspense every time that a baby might be on the way. In a world where everything is allowed yet no one desires anything—and desire has to be boosted with ever-stronger stimuli—let's just say that "Catholics do it better" with natural methods. The not-so-few who still trust the *Catechism of the Catholic Church* enjoy a much more fulfilling intimacy across the different seasons of married life. Admittedly, that physical connection also changes over the years, but that's just part of evolving together.

Finally, I must mention one last aspect. For whatever reason, people sometimes share with me their deepest, darkest secrets—secrets I truly never share with anyone, not even my husband. (Anyway, if I tried, he wouldn't listen; and if by chance he did, he'd forget immediately.) I know many people who struggle with sex—really quite a lot: impotence, frigidity, compulsive behaviors, you name it. There are marriages in which a couple goes years without making love. In talking with them, you almost always learn there were deep wounds—often in childhood or adolescence: emotional or physical abuse, violent parents, or neighbors or family friends who molested them, with mothers and fathers who turned a blind eye. Basically, if you can imagine it, it's probably happened. Obviously, I'm not equipped to unravel that huge mess of pain, which can trap people for years. I just want to say one thing I'm absolutely sure of: we're not capable of perfect love—not even for our kids, and we love them with all our hearts. Our hearts are just too small, incapable of the absolute love every one of us craves. Only a healed heart can create a fully beautiful, satisfying relationship—including a healthy sexual dimension. And only God can heal every wound of the heart. St. Thomas writes that before Original Sin, Adam and Eve experienced physical pleasure at a level higher than ours.

So let's ask for real help if there's trauma, pain, or abuse in the past. Encourage survivors to seek that help, because otherwise a marriage can end up thrown away for these reasons. But let's all ask God to give us a healed heart, one capable of both loving and accepting love—and to start anew at every moment, every day. Prayer is the only real aphrodisiac. Forget Viagra.

Chapter Three

Why Stay Married Even if ...
We're Different

"On Saturday I'd like to take you out to dinner. It will be exactly twenty-five years since our first positive pregnancy test."

"What's her name?"

"Whose?"

"Your lover's."

"I don't want a lover—imagine the effort of handling someone else besides you."

(I politely ignore the snarky tone.) "Chiquita? Morena? Rosita?"

(My husband's hypothetical lovers always have Spanish names, though occasionally a Svetlana or Ljudmila creeps in.)

Honestly, I've spent the last two years unsuccessfully trying to get him to invite me out to dinner—just the two of us. (That quick sandwich at the highway rest stop while we dash off to pick up a daughter doesn't count as a romantic evening.) I've asked him, hinted at it, suggested things, dropped jokes ... and *nothing*. My husband's response strategy is pure Virginia opossum: play dead. That's how he's survived all these years. Suddenly, out of nowhere, he invites me to dinner and even remembers the date of our first positive pregnancy test (he must have taken it well, evidently). He *has* to have another woman. Because my husband forgets appointments, birthdays (even his own, to be fair), anniversaries, our kids' school events, where he parked, people's names—everyone's except for the entire AS Roma lineup from the '73-'74 season onward, including the bench. He forgets absolutely everything and is allergic to any kind of celebration. To give you an idea, at *our* wedding, he showed up without a tie because he didn't want the ceremony to be too formal. So yes, it's quite natural that I'd suspect he's hiding something.

Now, I know I could have limited myself to simply replying, "That's a lovely idea, dear, thank you! We'll finally go out to dinner." But alas, I'm basically a nitpicker in life. I don't exactly "nag"—I *criticize*. If something's done right—like inviting me out for dinner—it could still be done better. In other words, "You should've done it sooner." There's always something missing, something to improve. It's my life's mission, carried out with tireless dedication. I do it with him, with the kids, with humanity at large.

I'm well aware that this is the main area where I need work, and I think it's where most women have to work on themselves: giving up the role of running the "Committee for a Better World" (credit John Gray), especially the part of the world we live in personally—which means, first of all, *improving the husband* and then the kids. Instead, we need to learn simply to welcome things as they are. Welcoming has the power to heal relationships, to untie knots, to close old wounds, to break the stalemate of conflicts that have festered for years. Unfortunately, only a woman who has truly felt welcomed—who has sensed the Father's gaze upon her—is capable of genuine welcome.

For instance, rejecting a man's input—maybe not even listening to his advice—has a huge negative effect on him, far worse than a woman being criticized by a man. Because the woman is like a mirror for the man; if she reflects a negative image of him, it hurts him more deeply than it would hurt her. She, on the other hand, craves his *love* more than his approval—someone to tell her she's beautiful. *He* wants her to confirm that he's "capable," that he's competent, that he has what it takes. (We mirror each other's thirst, in other words.) Sometimes you need to start by acknowledging each other's past histories, including family background. Embrace them, ask God to be present and to heal your spouse's history and your own, and never utter the kind of verdicts that kill: "You're just like your mother" or "You do that because your father ..."

The trouble is, at least some of the time, letting go of a critical gaze and learning a welcoming gaze—starting from a positive viewpoint of the other person: first and foremost, *I'm grateful you exist* and I see the good you bring to me, before focusing on flaws or mistakes—is a struggle. It demands a bedrock decision of the soul. It's a battle; men and women are as different as can be, so achieving communion, *"one flesh,"* is the hard-won outcome of heroic trench warfare, of a strenuous and total ascetic path, of a journey that's sometimes fun and sometimes maddening, uplifting, and depressing at the same time.

Me, for example, I can shift quite quickly from "Wow, how lucky I am" (like when I see my husband's integrity, intelligence, and moral compass) to "Why me?" (like when he's alone in the bedroom chatting animatedly with Rome's dedicated sports radio, or when sloth overtakes him and he tries not to do anything he's not strictly obliged to do—though in the end he does it anyway—or when he buys pointless, bulky kitchen gadgets, like a "potato comber" or a "pea sheller," that just clutter our tiny, 3x1-meter kitchen until cooking dinner becomes a Tetris-like puzzle: if you move two pots, you have to take down the chandelier. No wonder my artichoke purée often tastes like a high-school chemistry experiment. But he won't stop; whenever he sees "a thing that does something," he can't resist, the same way I can't say no to feathers and fringe.)

But if people had stuck to "We're just too different," no one would ever have come up with cheesecake or veal in tuna sauce. And truly, my husband and I might be the two most different creatures on the face of the Earth. Maybe one day God felt like making a bet with someone up in Heaven—maybe St. Rita, who's apparently in charge of impossible causes (indeed, when she was a nun, she made a dried stick bloom by watering it obediently out of love for her mother superior, and a rose eventually sprouted). I imagine He said, "Okay, Rita, if something good ever comes out of *these two*, I'll do something huge—*really* huge—to celebrate." (I'm hoping He decides to tackle humanity's leading crisis, i.e., water retention.)

In any case, true, profound communion between a man and a woman is like scaling an E11-grade[12] rock face—but it does lead to an amazingly beautiful summit. Because the spouse is the stand-in for the Other who is wholly Other. He's both the marker and the path to that Other. You can't get to Heaven except by going through your husband or wife—precisely *that* husband or wife. This is your path of conversion, the death of the old self that, for us married folks, must come from loving a being of another "species," someone who doesn't speak your language (or worse yet, doesn't speak at all, like my husband). And not just *some random person*, but *this* one here—who isn't actually a mistake, even on those days when you're convinced he might be. If you think he is a mistake, it's just a sign that you need to convert, because the other person's flaws only bother us when they resonate with

___
[12] The British E-grade is a system for measuring the difficulty of a rock climb. E11 is the highest grade on any climb in Britain.

something inside *us*. You can't claim to love God while you're stirring up fights with your husband or ignoring your wife.

I wrote a book on marriage, pretending I was offering girl-friends advice, when in reality I was trying to explain to myself the difficulties I faced in the early years of being a wife. Now it's been over twenty-five years, and for the latter half of that time—since I published my first book—I've met married men and women, people who are marriage-ready, and those who want to marry, divorce, or butcher each other, or just figure each other out; people feeling hopeless, in love, exhausted, stuck in a minefield of forbidden words and dead ends, but also unexpectedly propelled by sudden fresh starts. Couples dealing with an empty nest, couples taking their first steps, couples where both partners have faded away, turning into child-service agencies, and families where everyone thrives—including the spouses. I've learned a great deal I didn't know at first, and I've seen lives I never could've imagined. Let me give you a short summary of what I've discovered.

First off: men and women think differently. In the feminine world, everything is mysteriously interconnected; the male brain, on the other hand, separates information into compartments.

For instance, if I need to ask my husband where he's parked the car (the first available spot might be in some far-flung region of Italy, but hey, it's a lovely way to discover new cultures), I feel compelled to explain that I need it so I can go film a segment and "interview that priest I was telling you about the other day, but I also want to see Fr. Giuseppe, who wrote a great book on the prayer of the heart—did I mention we've been in touch? By the way, have you read that book about the starets[13] that Fr. Francesco

---

[13] A spiritual director or religious teacher in the Eastern Orthodox Church.

gave us? I think Eastern spirituality has a lot to teach us; anyway, we can talk later, so where is it?" And then my husband says, "Who?" because he has no idea what I'm talking about. Obviously, my original question — "Where's the car parked?" — got lost beneath all the extra info. The moment I mentioned the first priest, Guido basically switched off the audio. Meanwhile, for me, the flow of thought was perfectly logical. I've learned that I need to *close* one drawer — car parking — before opening another — interview — and another — priest who writes — and so on. If even one drawer remains open, my husband disappears: he turns on Radio Manà Manà[14] to debate De Rossi[15] with the hosts and figures he's done his conjugal duty by listening for those first two seconds. You see, a woman doesn't speak only to convey facts; she speaks to ask for or offer shared experience, to bring something into the collective pot. A man, for the most part, conveys just the facts. But I want him to show me that while he tells me where the car is, he also notices what an amazing woman I am, how impressive all my endeavors are, and how good my earrings look on me. (He's *aware* I have pierced ears, right?)

In truth, I don't actually *need* to ask where the car is parked. Ever since I caved in and got WhatsApp, we have a group chat called "Alzheimer Parking" in which the four licensed drivers in the house post only the location of whichever vehicle they used, sticking heroically to the bare minimum of words. The reason I ask is that I don't feel like checking the messages — I'd rather chat about what I'm doing. Like the Chinese cartographers in Borges' story who map everything in a 1:1 scale, we women do everything 2:1, meaning 1:1 plus commentary.

[14] Italian sports radio.
[15] Italian soccer (football) manager and former professional player.

Second pillar of the masculine mind: when something isn't working, that's the *only* thing a man can focus on—whether it's a failed DAZN sports stream, a messy legal brief, or a computer that's frozen. Don't bother him with any other issue, no matter how critical—like a daughter asking to spend the night at the home of people we've never met. I still haven't learned this basic marriage rule—"Don't speak to a man who's busy fixing something"—and so, seeing him standing there, I take the opportunity to unload all my parenting worries. In the spinning tunnel of maternal anxiety, thoughts pile up, entangle each other, and balloon until, as my husband tinkers with a cable, I'm jabbering away all by myself. By the time I've wound through enough twists and turns, my final verdict is that I'm a horrible mother who's made mistakes from preschool onward and that I'll never fix the damage. Typically my husband will then respond with something like, "Relax, it's the socket."

Another point: men don't want to talk about their problems; they want to be alone. They tackle one problem at a time. Women, meanwhile, see them all at once. A minor shift in work hours can become a chance to review not just the practical organization of the day but the entire child-raising method (which is pointless anyway—moms are always convinced they got everything wrong, except for those occasional "maternal pride" moments that can send us into a delirium of grandeur).

The male mind is tubular, processing one thing at a time; then, via culture and experience, men gradually add knowledge to that mental storehouse. In contrast, the female mind is cyclical, resetting once a month. For us, it's hard to accept anything as final, safe from reexamination. That's why when I start a conversation with, "I was also thinking that ..." my husband hurries out of the room to avoid reopening a decision already made—since, like most men, he's stuck in "energy-saving mode," and making decisions with a being from another species can be exhausting. And, as we know, once his battery is drained, the male mammal leaves "energy-saving mode" only by taking to the couch or doing something that lets his neurons spin freely at two miles an hour. For men, the biggest test in marriage is giving up that drive to conserve emotional energy. Accepting to lose one's life for another is the measure of how marriage challenges a man.

At that point, a man activates another wonderful mode: the "blank function" (registered trademark). It happens, for instance, when he's staring at the grout lines between floor tiles with an otherworldly intensity, and you start worrying he's rethinking your entire relationship—maybe he's plotting a fling with that total knockout, Ubalda—so you anxiously ask, "What are you thinking about?" If he replies, "Nothing," there's a good chance it really is *nothing*. (Never mind that Ubalda might be intriguing in her own right.) This "blank function" is a mirage for us women, who can be thinking about six things at once even when we sleep, but men need it to recharge.

By contrast, the female mind—rather than running on a single track—has four radar stations in the brain, like four different control towers. Our job is to dial those radars *down*, to avoid constantly reading into things or people. Often—indeed, very often—we need to avoid judging, analyzing, diagnosing. We have to try not to interpret everyone's words with a philological inquisition. The review board that operates inside my head is always in session, and my teenage daughters, now women in their own right, always bust me: "Okay, Mom, what do you find wrong with *her*?" "Who, me? Nothing at all, I swear!" "Why aren't you badmouthing her? Did you just go to Confession or something?" Sadly, God gave us teenage daughters precisely when we start feeling smug about being "good people." (They say, though, that the grandchildren they give you later will be your reward for not killing them.)

When a woman uses her "radar" on a man to interpret him, he feels intruded upon—because sometimes it *is* an invasion. Take gift-giving, for instance. If a man wants something specific—a particular camera, drill, or guitar—he might, out of responsibility, refrain from buying the top-notch version. *Love* means figuring out what he actually likes and going along with it. Modestly speaking, over the years I've given him guitars that are gorgeous but unplayable, books no one on Earth would want to read, cologne that triggers migraines, phone accessories that are incompatible with his actual phone—blithely ignoring the fact that loving someone can also mean patiently figuring out what he likes. In the case of men, that often entails the humility to ask rather than assume.

We also know that men's senses function differently than women's. One sniff inside the bedroom of two teenage boys and you'll lose all doubts that the male sense of smell is severely compromised. Nature does them a mercy by sparing them from their own fumes—it's pure survival. Then there's hearing. Again, for survival, men raise the threshold for detecting noise until it reaches precisely the point where they can sleep through an infant's midnight cries. Some men are born with this talent; others develop it over years of blasting The Police at eardrum-bursting volume or listening to endless radio replays of soccer matches. (Which, by the way, raises an interesting question: how can a man who's otherwise perfectly intelligent—or in my husband's case, downright brilliant—suffer through a replay hoping his team will win, when the match was years ago, and he knows perfectly well they lost? Let science figure that one out.)

Men's vision also has special quirks: as we know, they see moving objects better. Take underwear, for instance. If it's lying still in a drawer, it's basically invisible — unless a woman is wearing it, in which case it's not in the drawer at all. Probably the movement factor explains it; thanks to leftover caveman instincts for chasing down a running mammoth for dinner, men historically categorize moving creatures by edibility rather than by faces. Maybe that's also why my husband hardly greets any of our neighbors: none of them is edible, so he doesn't recognize them. If they were chickens, he'd undoubtedly be far more sociable.

Regarding sight, a man can usually recall a place years later, focusing on details I find mysterious, like architecture, topography, or the direction of a river. I have a vague awareness that different cities are traversed by different waterways, but for convenience I just mentally label all of them "the Tiber" — even in Paris there's a lovely "Tiber," for all I know. Most women see geography as a social convention. Personally, I avoid the chilly emptiness of official street names and label places with my memories: "Turn right where my old OB-GYN's office was when I was pregnant with Tommi," or "Go left where we rented that pony stroller."

Men's optic nerves also pick up only primary colors — everyone knows this. With the usual exceptions (artists, fashion designers, brand-new boyfriends in the first few days), men can't advise if your top is more "nude" or "pastel pink" — to them, it's all "pink," plus, "Wait, what's a top?" They basically just see colors to differentiate team jerseys and traffic lights: green means go, yellow means hurry up, red means you'd better stop, but if you're going to pull something sketchy, do it fast.

I could go on for hours about male/female differences, but I'd be as repetitive and tedious as the people who claim it's all just stereotypes. Here's what I really want to emphasize: the very differences that sometimes strain us so badly are not a design flaw. They're not something to erase or downplay. Marriage is fruitful precisely because it brings two people out of themselves, sending them on a path of conversion. By the sacrament, you bring into being the children of God, and the first two children are the man and the woman themselves, the spouses, who increasingly become sons and daughters of God by living within this difference—a difference that marriage forces them to grapple with. If actual children come from that union, wonderful. But the point is for the two of you, husband and wife, to undergo conversion, to become "one flesh." Let's remember: children aren't the *purpose* of marriage in a utilitarian sense that implies that the couple is entitled to children. That's one reason the Church opposes artificial fertilization: it holds that each life is sacred and untouchable from conception to natural death.

One of the goals of marriage is moving from living in the flesh to living as children of God. Our mutual differences and struggles aren't a reason to walk away; they confirm that the sacrament is saving you, killing off the old self. That's why Pope St. John Paul II advised not rushing into declaring a marriage null, because often it's the only laboratory in which we actually become Christian. In our bourgeois world, where social conflicts rarely break out into open brawls, only through extended, daily coexistence with others do we see how insane, selfish, and cynical we really are. And the only way to fix that is to have patience with one another.

The Lord really pushes us forward when we allow ourselves to let go—sometimes even letting go of tangible things. I've seen people break free just by giving away their collection of toy cars or books. When we surrender something—even reluctantly—God helps us take a leap. Letting go of pride, shrugging off people's negativity, accepting we're aging and losing our edge: that's when we climb faster toward the Lord, like rockets that shed parts the higher they go after takeoff.

Blessed Is the Day We "Got It Wrong"

Whenever there's a conflict between us and another person— starting with spouses—let's always remember the real problem is *us*. "Lord, grant me the grace to realize that I'm blind. Put Your mind in my heart. Let me see who I truly am." Once we glimpse the truth about ourselves, we get scared and lose all appetite for correcting the other person. Faith means being wary of ourselves, of our so-called "goodness," in order to cling to Jesus Christ. It means mistrusting—here I use the words of Fr. Emidio—our de- ceitful, babbling egos, who offer us a laughable pseudo-religiosity and put us on an endless quest for experiences and emotions, so that instead of really connecting with God, we end up stuck talk- ing to our superego, our childish, neurotic side. Faith isn't about obeying our superego; it's about going to meet others, forgiving them, recognizing they're as broke as we are.

In a family, we're always stepping on each other's toes, but that's exactly where we discover who we really are. We win people over to the Lord only by bearing with them when they're being difficult. And the family is the first place it happens. The King- dom of God is among us (this is the correct translation, rather than "within" us). Conversion is about sticking it out among others—especially our own household—while still carving out time for prayer. That's where we truly test ourselves on turning the other cheek and all those lofty ideals that seem so noble with strangers. But having to turn the other cheek to a teenage daughter who gets a thrill from calling you an old relic, or to a wife who always finds fault, is when we actually learn who we are. We discover parts of ourselves only conflict can reveal. If someone insults us, we should thank them, because they're giving us a free X-ray. Knowing our flaws, hearing the accusations thrown at us (after age twelve we can't dismiss them with "everyone's out to get me" or "they're just jealous"), is precious information—like building a database of what we lack. Once we grasp what a worm's nest we have inside, the Holy Spirit can come in, and the more our protective shell cracks, the more God's light shines through. The gentle guest of the soul then fills us, consoles us, and doesn't abandon us in His holy work of transformation, as St. Francis says. At that point, we can enter a fully satisfying dynamic of love—as long as we decisively renounce sin. I often make a ton of good resolutions in this area, then get distracted and, at the first opportunity, revert to old habits. A practical solution is to start right away by watching our words. Keep our mouths shut— "If you can't say anything nice, don't say anything at all"—and avoid criticism (which is about 90 percent of my usual conversation). Almost always, the best move is not to comment, not to say anything, even if it's true. Every so often, I try to justify it by saying, "I'm not badmouthing, I'm just describing," but that doesn't really cut it.

A good technique is to ask: *How would Mary speak?* People who have succeeded at this (not me) say that, contrary to popular belief, words can shape our thoughts as much as thoughts shape our words. The typical teenage notion—that thought alone controls words (see Descartes, Marx, Hegel, etc.)—misses the mark. The childlike thinking of our age says we're ruled by emotions and whims (hence the erroneous mind-body split taught by gender ideology, which is a rejection of the objective limits of reality—but that's another huge topic). Yet if we want to follow Jesus (and *want to* is the key), we need to crucify some of our impulses, telling ourselves no.

We can't change most of what we think, but we *can* change our words. After a few days of guarding our speech—and therefore our thoughts—our way of acting changes too. Our leprosy is made of pointless overthinking, mental babble. Neither intuition nor the heart gets us anywhere. The answer is Jesus' Passion—He goes to die for us. Christianity is flesh and blood. If we pay full attention to every aspect of our vocation, we won't have time to sin; the devil won't know where to find a foothold. We shouldn't have a spare moment for anything except our particular calling. If we're married, our path to God is through the kids, the husband, the mother-in-law. Some people, because they don't love anyone, think they love God—like Charles Péguy wrote. The more we're rooted in real life, dealing with annoying or ill-mannered folks, the closer we draw to God.

And when we encounter Him—maybe in a moment of grace, one of those unexpected breakthroughs He sometimes grants—we have to cultivate the relationship properly. We need to learn to speak with Him, to listen, or He'll bow out politely. He doesn't want to impose His presence. That's why prayer is primarily trying to convince Him that we truly, freely desire Him. When He calls, we run to Him; we pray without ceasing to understand His will—even though, when she was in preschool, my daughter once told me, "Pway all the time? Sowwy, I can't, I has too many things to do." (Maybe once we're past preschool, we have fewer demands.) If we do manage to pray, we find out that to fully convert, we have to deal with things we normally wouldn't care about. Because we—and this is the crux of Christianity—are fundamentally critical, complaining, and judgmental. We're structurally unable to do good even though we can see it. That's why we have to subject our nature to the Cross, entering into Jesus' logic. Otherwise, we won't see Him, won't meet Him. And our ego deflates first and foremost by asking God, declaring that we're fundamentally incapable, begging Him to smash our hearts (He literally cracked St. Philip's ribs) and then to clothe us in humility, to put up with us, to forgive us. If we start doing that, Jesus is persuaded, and one day—after a push here, a shove there—He graces us. He tears away a piece of ourselves and replaces it with Himself.

Some people—even those on a faith journey—don't want that. You can't force them to see it. We get tempted by looking for miracles, or by seeking power in the Church, or by spirituality, novenas, and pious devotions (which can help, but they're not the goal). The core of Christianity is the Cross, and there's no escaping it. Until we take it up, we're not Christians. The only option is the meat grinder: letting the old, problematic, absurd self die. When everyone exploits you and takes advantage of you, that crazy side of you dies, and you heal. And you *give your life.*

Christianity is a person—Jesus—who makes life possible for others, who becomes the servant of the Lord, taking on other people's burdens unfairly. Neither miracles nor healings alone changed people for good. It took the Cross for even His closest followers to understand. If we want to call ourselves by His name—Christians—then we too must carry burdens that aren't our own. Ideally in silence, unlike me, who feels like blasting social media with a post for every shirt I iron, because the world ought to know. And because I'm aspiring to the title of Mother of the Year, I'm always up for dropping off and picking up daughters and friends—yet humbly, I'd like each trip recorded on a funerary monument encrusted with rubies, placed over my grave. (Since the sculpture isn't ready yet, I simply tell my kids about it. Not to make them feel guilty, of course.)

I know plenty of people who, unlike me, carry big burdens quietly. They're wise, because anger and gossip ruin everything, even for those who bear a lot. Yet our eternal destiny is decided in the family, by shouldering both our own load *and* others', without complaining. The more sincere and committed we are in that, the more the Lord steps in and changes things.

Blessed Is the Day We "Got It Wrong"

One last decisive secret: When your wife or husband does something that annoys you, don't take it out on *them*. Argue with the Lord who put that person at your side. We're all flawed, half-insane—but Jesus chose to show His risen Self first to the most offbeat person of all, Mary Magdalene. We become functional only when we say yes to God. It's hot, there are lines, mosquitoes everywhere, but we say, "Yes, God, I accept it." Martyrs used to get it over with all at once; we have to do it bit by bit. (In Luke's Gospel, "cross" isn't a random metaphor—He's talking about the struggle of day-to-day living.)

Then God arrives and loves us so personally that it's shocking. He'll make real, concrete things happen. He wants to stir up our jealousy, wants us to love Him above everything else, just as He loves us.

So for those of us who find family life both beautiful and challenging, it's an unparalleled opportunity. We can give away what we don't even possess—light, hope, joy. We can tend to others' problems, act without expecting anything in return, learn the others' language, accept being loved in a way different from how we love. Every day there's a bit of desert to cross, a disappointment, an unmet need. That's the exact place and time for us to meet Him. Not tomorrow, not in another life story, not with different people, not with a more "loaded" husband (who, for instance, has a working auditory channel) or a kid who hasn't decided to test the endurance of our coronary arteries. No—right here, right now, in this life we've been given. It's the perfect one for us.

Chapter Four

Why Stay Married Even if ...

Cheating Seems to Be the Solution

It's three in the morning and I'm wide awake—which, sadly, is nothing new. It's more like a defining trait of my life. When I was younger, 3 a.m. usually meant cramming last-minute for a chemistry or biology test (my brain rejects all scientific information, so I had to literally glue it in place right before go-time) or maybe hitting the clubs. Then came the years of staying up to breastfeed and soothe colicky babies, followed by the era of writing books and clearing out an inbox the size of Mount Everest. And now? Now I'm just trying to remember my own name and where I stashed that social security form—plus my glasses, and then the form again, which I've apparently set down in the fridge while searching for a yogurt that wasn't *too* expired. But mostly, at this unholy hour, my core business is loading and unloading the washing machine. I do it nonstop, yet my kids still manage to fling jokes about how long their T-shirts take to reappear in the closet, washed and ironed. ("So when exactly am I getting my green Carhartt back? I threw it in the laundry along with my chainmail right after the Battle of Montaperti ...")

Anyway, it's because of these nocturnal laundry adventures that I catch Sara's message in real time. At three in the morning, she's asking me to pray for Maddalena. And I get a bad feeling. She doesn't say why, but I suspect what I've been dreading for

71

a while: a full-blown marital crisis. I've been hearing from Maddalena for years, not super often, but regularly—every three or four months. She's always told me about her husband's depression, his low income, the fact that he no longer travels for work and borrows money from his mom (who's now *way* too involved in their family life—yikes), plus they found out one of the kids has serious health issues. Every year, the picture she paints looks gloomier. The last time I spoke to her, she said, "Pray for me, because I can't do it anymore." And ever since then, I've been worried. If you quit praying just when you're stuck in the desert of hard times, temptation is *definitely* going to come knocking. I know that sometimes praying feels harder than chopping wood or mopping up after a group of teenagers who partied, got drunk, and threw up everywhere (which ranks slightly worse than working in a coal mine). It might look like nothing, but it's the hardest work in the world, because it means stopping whatever you're doing—physically *and* mentally—snatching up your head and heart from whatever's devouring them, and pointing them in a different direction.

I'm worried about Maddalena because, in the massive struggle she's going through, she needs a source of nourishment. When you give so much for so long, you need a spring to drink from that can revive you. This goes for everyone, men included—but especially for us women, who tend to place our security outside ourselves. Prayer is a woman's soul. A woman who doesn't pray is a woman with no life left in her. Having a rosary in your pocket is the fountain of security because it helps measure our fickleness and our fears. We try to repeat the Hail Mary more and more attentively, feeling each word, while going through the mysteries and remembering the story that saved our lives and can save anyone who asks.

Our Lady is the best psychoanalyst around (and she's free). We're anxious, insecure, and unstable because we don't lean on her and, through her, on the Savior—on the One who can rescue us from fear, selfishness, neurosis, all those giant messes we risk creating multiple times a day. Prayer washes your brain, helps you see clearly, opens new horizons, puts you back in your proper place, and gives you the grace to accept yourself for who you are so you can become who you're meant to be.

You don't pray *because* you have faith; you pray *in order to have* faith. Whether someone has faith or not, prayer finds its own path: it's a light that illuminates, that walks, that grows, that purifies, that calms the storm, that declutters your brain and your memory. You can't run away from your own conscience—everything you need to know is written there. Little by little, prayer leads you to become the person you truly are. It guides you inside yourself, where the light is, where you can rest in joy. And from there, you get the impulse to act, to make real choices that would be unthinkable without prayer.

I jot down an "M" on the back of my hand—my infallible digital organizer—to remind myself to call her in the morning. When I do, she picks up in tears. I could pretty much tell her what she's about to confess: a cute coworker showed up, offered her a chocolate, and told her she looked tired. "Do I have dark circles?" "No, not at all—you have gorgeous eyes." There are moments of vulnerability when, for a woman, simply *being seen* is huge. It can become everything. One day it's a compliment, the next it's a witty remark, then it's a croissant left on your desk for breakfast, then a bit of praise for your work in front of everyone at the staff meeting. These are things you normally wouldn't even notice if you're not hooked on other people's approval. But when your love tank is running on fumes, when real closeness with your husband has fizzled, a teeny-tiny drop of water disappears in a second—and you instantly want more because it reactivates sensors you were sure had dried up forever.

Over the phone, Maddalena is sobbing, but if I try to tell her she's making a huge mistake, she insists that she's never felt better and doesn't need my advice. So I gather the situation's already gone too far. The time for sweet nothings, flirty texts, and that first thrilling chill has come and gone. She admits it's already beyond that point, and it happened fast. No rose, no sweet little book with a heartfelt dedication, no suggestive comments on her social media pics: they've already ended up in bed. And he's already gone into detail about how he and his wife have been "done" for ages (the classic line). Honestly, you'd be surprised how many of these serial cheaters claim they are "done." Then you find out the wife's pregnant again, "But that was only the one time, I swear!" Now the cute coworker is already feeding her promises about their future together—forever—just not *right away*, because "it's not the right time" (another classic).

I have no idea how to get her to backpedal. I decide to appeal to her jealousy, because right now, it's all about hormones—a tidal wave of testosterone and estrogen calling the shots. (A friend of mine, who's a friar, used to say the hormone zone lasts about eighteen months for men and thirty-six for women, starting from their first sexual encounter, which sets the timer ticking.) I'm afraid no normal argument appealing to common sense, her genuine love for her husband, or even her faith will make a dent at the moment. Less than zero chance. So I try, at least, to get her to see that a guy who sleeps with you after a few days—who's married, who's already made it clear his family is off-limits—might not be the pinnacle of faithful, starry-eyed romance. But, hey, lust is sneaky: it'll tell you any lie to get what it wants—some sex, some tenderness, some illusions—and it doesn't care how many bodies it leaves behind, starting with those of her two innocent children.

So I go for the jealousy angle over his wife. I tell Maddalena that she'll always be the second choice. Christmas, holidays, the major moments—she'll have to disappear and let him go back to his picture-perfect family. "And that's okay with you, Maddalena? That your great families both remain *so perfect*? You're fine with this weird little arrangement, the tacky motel nights, with him lowering his voice whenever he calls his wife? With you making up excuses to your husband and living in constant fear of being found out, but unable to resist replying to that coworker's texts?"

But really, what I want to tell Maddalena is that she's out of her mind, that she's throwing away something real and huge for a lie. I want to tell her she's being an idiot, that this is a catastrophic mistake, that her husband is a difficult man going through a difficult time—and yes, sure, it's gone on for years, but those years of carrying a heavy load have crushed him precisely *because* he's a serious man who wants to take care of his family. Think about it, Maddalena: he would never do this to you, but your coworker is doing it to *his* wife, so do you really think he won't eventually do the same to you if you become the "official" woman in his life? (Which, as he's basically told you, is never going to happen anyway.)

The illness of your child, financial troubles, your husband's personality, all of his and your emotional baggage—it's a lethal cocktail. Then that "cute coworker" smelled easy prey, realized it would be a cinch, and lit the match that set everything off. Meanwhile, for him, this is just his lifestyle: you're not the first, you won't be the last. And what will you be left with in the end?

Unfortunately, I suspect that thinking about how much pain this is causing and will cause her children might not really matter to her right now. She sees only her own needs—she's blinded. I know she'll regret this eventually because she's a good mom who loves her kids. In a little while, when she sobers up from this hormonal binge, she'll be heartbroken about what she's done—but the problem is, by then, who knows if it'll be too late to save her children from the fallout of a separation.

Sara and I promise to pray for her, although that's something I'm careful about promising unless I'm certain I can follow through. I don't want to kid anyone, least of all God. So I have to be selective about who I pray for—kind of like a hospital triage nurse, giving priority to "red codes" (real ones, not the never-ending list of lethal tumors my friend Raffa thinks she has. At the slightest bump on her neck, she's begging me to adopt her husband in exchange for the many purses she'll bequeath to me upon her imminent demise). So we're going to pray, because I don't think there's anything else I can do for Maddalena right now. She's not listening to anyone. I'm not going to tell her husband, either—I don't feel entitled to betray a secret that she entrusted to me. (It'd be a different story if I'd discovered it on my own.) Besides, even if he confronted her now, I don't think anything could stop her. Sadly, this isn't the first time I've had someone confess an affair to me, and I've never been able to stop them. I've tried everything: cussing them out, coaxing them, just listening, but if that decision doesn't start within the person who's being tested, nothing you say can fix it.

When someone cheats, they build a flimsy house-of-cards narrative about their life, told through an accuser's lens. I've never yet heard someone in the heat of the moment say, "Wow, I'm a total jerk. I've done something truly horrible to the people who love me the most. I broke my word, their trust, and my kids' hearts." Nope. Instead, they're all calm and convinced they finally deserve what they should have had all along: "I've put up with so much up to now; I've been so strong. This is life finally giving me a chance, and I'd be crazy not to take it, because maybe it's my last." The alternative, they insist, is an eternal prison sentence: a miserable life alongside a terrible person. Telling someone who's in that mindset, "Hey, if you don't blow up what you've already built, eventually the sun *will* shine again. One day you'll be grateful you stuck it out, that you didn't toss away something so precious," is completely pointless. They won't hear you if they don't *want* to.

There's only one way out: realizing that *we* are the problem. And if I'm the problem, who can fix me? In the end, it's not about how my husband or wife behaves, and it's definitely not about the attention of some fling. Only someone bigger than me can fix me. In other words, only God.

Our only solution is to shout to God from the bottom of the pit: really saying, "Help me," and starting an honest relationship with Him. If that honest relationship is missing—and for many of us, it is—our faith is chaos, hypocrisy, a giant mask. Then come the tough times (Lent, or any real cross to bear), which is our chance to realize that we're the problem. That's the moment you can choose to rebel and run away, or to become true friends with the Lord. After that, all your relationships blossom, and everyone settles down.

Most people think it's always someone else's fault. The antidote to that mindset is the Bible, which shows us how to face our situations by God's rules, not ours. Look at Susanna, who entrusted her cause to God; or Esther, who accepted her lot and offered it up for her people; or Joseph, who endured his brothers' hatred but kept doing his best wherever he was sent, never nursing resentment. By putting Someone else's Word in place of our nonsense, emotions, and hormones, we can start living eternal life right now. It changes us; it makes things happen.

Blessed Is the Day We "Got It Wrong"

And that's when miracles happen, Maddalena. I wish I could drill that into your stubborn, lovely little head. Miracles are God's serious response to those who seriously call out to Him. Choose to remain in your story—which, yes, is painful and huge and complicated, I get it. But if you decide to stay put and ask God to help you, He *will* step in, and you'll find paradise right here on earth. When our hearts are all-in, He responds. As Fr. Emidio used to say, if something's not working, it's usually because we're all scattered inside, torn up like pulled pork, not even sure what we're asking for, full of contradictions—like me when I pray for a friend in financial trouble. I leave church aflame with charity, swearing off every little personal purchase so I can support him. Then I walk ten steps and stick to a store window like a gecko because of a face cream that's $199. (No, I don't buy it, but the problem is that I've even *considered* it.) Or when you pray for your son's exam and solemnly promise to recite St. Bridget's prayers for the next twelve years—but after the exam goes well, on day three (with only about 4,380 days to go) you're telling yourself God isn't such a stickler. Come on, He's not an accountant, is He?

So first step—for Maddalena and for every one of us—is deciding, for real, what's important. If we can unite our brains and hearts, then we're set. We must ask Christ to keep us near His heart and fix our gaze on Him, because if we focus on ourselves, we freeze up. But if we look at Him, we can truly change. Of course, we can't *make* that happen. All we can do is *ask*.

Second step: patience. Always. Patience with others—especially our kids. (Should you ever feel an irrational surge of enthusiasm for life, drop by my daughters' room after I haven't checked it for a few hours and see if you can even spot the floor, covered in Victoria's Secret bodysuits, stuffed bears from preschool, dirty underwear, clean sweaters, ancient Greek dictionaries, marshmallows with hair stuck to them, medical certificates I've been hunting for twenty days, and four-year-old concert tickets.) And show the same patience with yourself, too, because things happen gradually. Only then can we start a journey, a holy pilgrimage, and there's no point trying to be "perfect." We're not stoic philosophers. All we're asked to do is cling to Christ with everything we've got, like branches to a vine. If we stick close to Him, everything else follows. That's why, at the point Maddalena's reached—head over heels for someone else, basically loathing her husband—there's no sense in offering typical marriage advice tidbits, like "Oh, make sure you two go out alone," or "Don't start complaining the second he steps through the door," or "Maybe save those TMI digestive updates for someone else at bedtime." She's way beyond the old-auntie advice stage (my specialty). Her life is at a crossroads. It's one of those brutal tests where you decide whether to live for yourself and your so-called feelings or to live according to your Baptism, nailing those wrong desires to the Cross. Long story short, you decide if you're going to be a Christian.

I don't judge her weakness. The life this coworker is showing her looks so sparkly, airy, and thrilling, while her real life—the only actual, concrete one—is objectively heavy. She has a sick child, little money, a marriage battered by trials, and a husband who seems weak and defeated by their troubles, and who's now turning paranoid and jealous as soon as he suspects the coworker's existence (which makes him even less appealing). In other words, it's a trap with no obvious escape. What they need is friends who form a protective barrier around them, and they need a ton of prayer. But first and foremost, they need a *decision*. And Maddalena's already made the opposite one—she's surrendered, ready to dive headfirst into this relationship with the coworker. She's chosen what she hopes will be a second shot at youth, but all it's guaranteed to do is plunge her kids and husband into despair.

Then again, she could turn it around—save herself and them. You can't just quit because something's hard. "It's too hard" is never a valid objection to doing what's right. (I'm not sure who said that, but I'd like to carve it into every school entrance, the city gates, every doorway in the world.) When something is hard, we should take it as a sign that we're on the path to salvation. When a woman realizes that the family is a workshop, that's when her husband and kids catch on, too, and everything at home changes. That's when the real miracle of conversion happens, which makes alchemy's lead-into-gold look like a cheap knockoff. That's when you start living an entirely new life.

The road is Christ. So you stay calm, you talk less—*much* less!— and just by living your daily life, you find God. Paradise is when you meet Him and start to look like Him, when you stop seeing Him as an enemy, when your "good" and "bad" aren't decided by *your* intelligence but by His love.

Right now, Maddalena is judging her life story on her own terms: she's decided for herself what's good—this fling—instead of trusting the promise God made to her and her husband. But in the end, faith demands us to ask a question: Do I go with my own impulses—feelings, random thoughts, spontaneous instincts—or do I cling to the solid rock of faith?

We must rely on faith to lead us because we're inherently contradictory. We don't do the good we want to do; we do the evil we swore we wouldn't. It's like we have two boxers inside us—one is in God's image, and the other is a total demon, fueled by cursing, bullying, and manipulative double-talk.

For example, if something about someone else annoys me, it's because I'm *worse* than they are, or else their behavior wouldn't rub me the wrong way—it'd just bounce off ("*ce rimbalza*,"[16] as the Romans say). If it gets under my skin, that's a sign I need to change *myself*. My husband's so good-hearted that he rarely notices malice in others, whereas I love to keep a full dossier on everyone, Stasi-style.[17] But, hey, "forgive seventy times seven," "turn the other cheek"—those apply at home, not just on the bus. And here, women are the catalysts who set everything in motion; it all starts with us. For me, for instance, the hardest part of having a family is that I can't throw temper tantrums whenever I feel like it, because I know my bad mood will spill over onto everyone else. But the flip side is also true: living family life well can transform your home into the best place to be, and that vibe is contagious. Yes, sometimes—like in Maddalena's case—it demands a really tough decision. But it's worth it.

Sure, friend, if you decided to engage in this battle, you'd probably feel crushed by an insane amount of effort: giving up this man might seem like the biggest sacrifice of your life, and no one would even notice. But we know there's a good Father who sees every little sacrifice, every text you decide *not* to answer, every compliment you let fall flat. Each of those yeses you say to your real life sends angels into a standing ovation. This goes for all of us: what we do echoes in eternity, even the small, so-called mediocre things we do that cost a huge amount of effort and remain in the shadows. (Nobody's rolling out the red carpet

[16] Literally, "it bounces," a saying that basically equates to the English school rhyme, "I'm rubber, you're glue; whatever you say bounces off me and sticks to you." Or rather, to brush something off as completely meaningless.
[17] The Ministry for State Security, commonly known as Stasi, was East Germany's state security service and secret police from 1950 to 1990.

because you didn't snap at someone or because you handed over the money you would've spent on your eighteenth black T-shirt to help a struggling family—and nobody will roll it out for you, Maddalena, if you turn down what feels like the love of your life.)

Which is why, in these test moments, we really have to learn how to pray. We're blind—and we don't even know we're blind. We ask for the wrong things, often things that actually harm us. We ought to stop begging for those four cents of affection and start asking for the fullness of it. Ask boldly, with trust and perseverance, to be healed deep down, and to live your life like a piece of art, carefully crafted—because there are no insignificant lives or minor details. God gives Himself entirely in every moment, even in the small stuff of each day.

If only I could make you see that, Maddalena! I'd tell you that when you cling to the Lord, you feel like dancing with Him, and you somehow guess the dance He likes best. As Madeleine Delbrêl wrote, you dance with Him through your workday, through heatwaves, through freezing cold. Then you're not crushed when things are less than perfect; you don't let yourself get suffocated. And if someone bumps into you, you can smile about it, joining the universal music of God's love. Of course, sometimes I myself experience that lovely dance-with-God feeling, but then something happens that reminds me who I truly am—like the time an elderly lady at the checkout asked if she could go in front of me because she "just has these few items," i.e., a basket with butter and a single zucchini. Meanwhile, she's spent a good chunk of time chatting away with a spry seventy-year-old sporting purple hair. Clearly, she's got *zero* pressing engagements in her life, while I've been on my feet for thirteen hours and still have about six more to go, plus I have to pick my daughters up from a birthday party, and one of them is bringing a friend home to sleep over, which means a Tetris round of inflating mattresses and switching sheets in our tiny, overstuffed house—right after I cook dinner, put things away, fold the usual piles of laundry, and answer ten messages. In that moment, the Stalin in me just wants to say, "No, you can't cut in, you slowpoke with your single zucchini—if you don't move, I'll whack you in the femur with my cart." So much for my half-whispered Rosary—clearly, I've still got some personal growth to do.

But Maddalena might be miles ahead of me. Because conquering a temptation like the one she's facing—giving up what feels like the most wonderful thing she's ever had or ever will—is one massive leap of faith. It's taking on the risk that staying in her marriage might mean losing the one she believes is her true soulmate. In middle-class life, there's always an airbag; you're insured for everything. But if you stay small and faithful, willing to lose this so-called "golden opportunity," then the Lord becomes your defender and even handles the fine details. He doesn't remove our problems and struggles; He hops into the boat with us, and in the end, thanks to Him, we make it. When He sees people who are sincere, God can work miracles like it's nothing.

Fr. Emidio often shared stories of people who came to his confessional asking for money or other help but who never actually wanted to change. Then one day, a young woman who badly needed help came in, but she was offering *him* money—a donation she'd received. She insisted on working for her income rather than begging. That was it; Fr. Emidio called in favors and found her a job. In the same way (yes, I'm repeating it for emphasis), when God sees people who are sincere, He can work miracles like it's nothing. God isn't moved by fancy formulas but by our sincerity. If we're truly unified inside, if we're real, we touch God's heart. Most of the time, we're not. We hold back. The real prayer is: "Help me change."

Blessed Is the Day We "Got It Wrong"

So Maddalena, you can simply say to God, "I can't give up my coworker—it's stronger than I am. But I *do* want to fight, so help me conquer my own heart." That prayer *always* gets heard, but it's also the one we almost never say.

Usually, we treat Christianity like we expect God to hand us good health, money, bulletproof security—stuff that has zero to do with Christ, who didn't exactly have a glamorous career, if you glance at that symbol we often wear around our necks. It's like those folks on a pilgrimage that a certain priest once told me about: instead of accepting whatever their spiritual journey had to offer, they cherry-picked what they wanted out of it. One little old lady took only the bus rides and spent the rest of the time at the hotel pool. Another guy could never be roused from bed. An old man was constantly running late. Three girls joined in the hopes of finding a husband.

But real grace isn't when God bows to our insane demands. Real grace is when He helps us become adults—when He teaches us to walk on our own feet, to stand firm. In short, to stay anchored in reality. I'm hoping so much that Maddalena will find her way. It's not too late.

Chapter Five

Why Stay Married Even if ...
He Cheated on Me

By the end of almost every public event I hold, I witness the grand establishment of an official fan club. Too bad it's always named after my husband, not me. Yet I could've sworn I'd just spent the last two hours exhaustively describing his flaws and talking about the patience and nobility of heart with which I attempt to improve him.

But the truth is, alongside all my husband's shortcomings—which, to the male listeners, only inspire a sense of camaraderie—his many virtues (yes, I must admit it) shine so brightly that they're obvious even to those who don't know him. And, in fact, I agree with them—there's a reason I married him. I did it with the aim of elevating him to a more advanced model (you know, from Husband-14 to Husband-15+, so to speak).

Among the many positives of Husband-14, even before his upgrade to 15+, the one I treasure the most is definitely that I trust him—indeed, I trust him more than I trust myself. A total, unshakable trust, despite the fact that I just finished grilling him about an orange mark on his shirt collar—clearly, in my assessment, lipstick. (He didn't even bother to look; from the couch he decreed, "It's more likely tomato sauce." Excuse me, what do you mean *"more likely"*?) But despite those paranoid spells, I genuinely know I can trust him. And I don't just mean sexual fidelity, but loyalty in general.

It's something I couldn't do without. Yet I've seen with my own eyes that marriage can be stronger even than disloyalty. It can stay alive (or even rise again) after crossing the line—beyond the supposed point of no return. I can't begin to grasp how people accept that stage when, on their own, they have to love for two. It's beyond reason to believe that such a moment—however long it lasts—is just a phase. Or to believe that, even if it never passes, the marriage can still remain a marriage forever, and that a wounded heart can keep beating. It requires a huge heart—something double its normal size, strong enough to endure. It's the kind of heart found in those left behind who remain faithful to a spouse who's started a new life. Such people exist, unbelievable though it seems, and they're not living on Mars. But you need the certainty that you are within a greater love if you're truly to forgive and seriously reboot the marriage, to rebuild real communion.

It's *communion* that's difficult because, sure, you can stay together. That's doable. But maybe you carry a savage, repressed resentment, full of muttered undercurrents and biting remarks. Or you can look the other way in order to maintain a comfortable life—like the wives of wealthy husbands who are perpetually "distracted" yet provide comfort and a home inside the limited-traffic zone. (Yes, they're out there, I know some personally.) You can stay together for the kids' sake, forgiving a wife who's decided to return, *meaning* it sincerely, but without being able to overcome your bitterness. It's stronger than you. Or you might settle for a separate life under the same roof—no outright fights but also no joy. Or again, you could forgive your husband's affair but constantly reassert your primacy as the "legitimate woman," the one who gets the last word over the benchwarmer. Like the woman I know who took back the man who'd been cheating on her for years. He practically had a second family with a younger partner—and he even had a child with her. When that other woman died unexpectedly, the wife welcomed him back home full-time, but she made him give the child up for adoption and forbid him from seeing him for years (only on her deathbed did she tell their older children they had a half-brother). Then people wonder why I don't write novels: I could never invent something so extreme; it would sound too far-fetched. For clarity's sake, I understand all those people whose stories pass in front of my eyes while I'm writing here. They all seem very human to me. Forgiving a fling or a head-over-heels romance, forgiving the person to whom you gave yourself wholly and unreservedly, loving the child your husband had with another woman ... it must be an ordeal. Every cell of that child reminds you of your man being with someone who wasn't you. It's tough, I get it, even though that child is blameless. But the point for me is that the real issue isn't simply *staying* but *rebuilding communion*—or forging a new communion that perhaps wasn't there before.

A priest who spent the second half of his life more or less confined to the confessional once told me that from his long experience, he'd learned that in the case of hormone-crazed cheating, the main strategy is to hold on until it passes. Among his spiritual daughters, two had gone through that trial at the same time. One yelled, screamed, badmouthed her husband to all her friends, and threw dishes (which, if you ask me, is a fairly measured reaction; I'd be chucking garbage cans). The other, however, tried following the gospel. She radically changed her behavior, and when her husband came back to her—partly thanks to her gentleness—she took him back in. Today the man practically worships his wife.

Blessed Is the Day We "Got It Wrong"

In every season of life, and so in marriage as well, we can choose to respond in a purely human way or in a *baptized* way. And I'd say betrayal is where the difference between these two responses becomes most obvious and dramatic. *Humanly speaking*, when you're betrayed, your only option is to walk away, hate, or harbor resentment or vengeance. But those who live as baptized—whose central relationship in life is with the Lord—can see adultery in a different light, namely as a path to conversion (though it's certainly still painful).

I mentioned that for me, trust is paramount, so I can't imagine how people do it. I, who sniff my husband's sweaters for extrafamilial hairs and get irritated even by his *past*—I'm not thrilled he dared to exist before meeting me. Sure, he could *exist*, but he had no business interacting with any other females, not even his preschool classmates. When we watch a film together, if a Scarlett Johansson appears in a three-square-inch bra, he's already been well-trained to show no sign of appreciation. If I say, "Wow, she's gorgeous," he's drilled to respond something like, "Eh, I don't know, look at those thick ankles." (Random nonsense, because let's face it, if you're looking at Scarlett in lingerie, you don't notice her ankles at all.)

So personally, I have no clue how people manage it, but I've met individuals who, confronted with infidelity, have *transformed* themselves. I've said it before: our interior system is "crazy." Call it wounded, call it the old self—whatever label we slap on it, it needs healing, and God's Word is there to do exactly that. Change happens when your head says one thing but the gospel says something else, and you opt for the gospel way. Our subconscious takes over when we let emotions drive our soul. But sometimes, someone manages to discover how not to tune in to the anger we all carry inside. Saints don't *lack* that anger; they just learn not to give in to it, to put their wild subconscious in check. St. Francis, for example, was an elegant, wealthy party-goer—in modern terms, he might have owned a place in Chelsea or Manhattan, or maybe just in Parioli.[18] He was his dad's son, a lover of luxury and the finer things, with an artist's temperament: creative, brilliant. And *he* decided to hug and kiss the leper, the person everyone was revolted by, who couldn't come near the city center because he stank so badly. That was the moment Francis broke all remaining resistance to God. The gospel is like alchemy, turning lead into gold: with him, the experiment succeeded. He became a new creation, one that would change history more than most.

My friend Elisabetta told me she trusted her husband completely—hence, being mentally balanced (unlike me), she never checked on him, never sniffed his clothes, and never pictured exotic mistresses whenever he spent extra time at the hardware store. But it was his mistress who called Elisabetta out of the blue and spilled everything, because he, following the most clichéd script, had promised that mistress something like, "Oh, my wife and I are over, we just share a bed like brother and sister, if only I'd met you before, we'll spend next Christmas together, I'll leave her and marry you," *blah blah blah.* When Elisabetta got that phone call, she was in the car on her way to pick up one of their kids from violin class. She had to pull over, get out, and throw up by the roadside, doubled over. She triggered her emergency plan, sending Grandma to pick up the budding violinist and his two sisters, then told everyone she was having one of her disabling migraines and locked herself in her room, where she cried and vomited for hours, unable to talk to anyone. Her husband was off on a business trip—who knew if it was with the mistress or

[18] An upscale Roman neighborhood.

not? And right then, her old clay-court tennis resilience kicked in, the stamina for making it through matches that drag on forever. When you're exhausted and about to lose, you focus the last of your strength on what's strictly necessary and let everything else go. (For example, when I run, I have no idea where I am; I can't see a thing because I'm channeling everything into staying alive. I don't admire the scenery, and, unfortunately, I don't spot potholes, steps, roots, or lampposts either. Oh well, scraped knees apparently keep you looking youthful, giving off a certain preschool vibe that suits me.) Elisabetta did the same: she dedicated herself to surviving. She stayed utterly clear-headed; she told me that in those hours, she kept saying to herself, "If he's sick of me, a hysterical outburst won't make him stay. You can't *force* love. I won't trap him with guilt or threats. I won't use our kids as a form of blackmail. I want to be loved, and I want to love him. I want him saved, I want him truly happy. I know I can't be happy without him. But if I want him back, screaming is useless."

I need to find out which drug this woman was on, because she showed superhuman strength. "Don't think I prayed a ton at that moment," she told me. "Night came, then the next day, and I couldn't even manage a Hail Mary. I just kept repeating, 'Jesus, you handle it,' or maybe just 'Jesus.' The grandparents took the kids to school, so I had a few more hours to line up my thoughts, shower, pull on a tracksuit, and go pick them up. In the meantime, I formed my plan. Which was no plan at all. When he got home from the trip two days later, I told him straight up: that his mistress had called me, that I knew everything I needed to know, that I didn't need the details because they'd only make me feel worse, that I loved him and was willing to forgive and welcome him back, but I'd be waiting for him to return to me with an undivided heart, not one that was fifty-percent mine. And meanwhile, I'd do my best not to take revenge or have fits in front of the kids, because a pity-based or forced love is worthless to me."

Her husband was left feeling like a boxer who'd just taken a punch to the chest. He couldn't breathe normally for hours. And that kicked off months of him living two separate lives. On one side, he had the younger colleague with whom he traveled and had business dinners and after-dinner liaisons with lacy underwear (so maybe we women can't park well, but we sure know how to slip a bra out through the sleeve of our sweater in public, which throws men for a loop)—and dramatic scenes, because even her tell-all phone call hadn't managed to yank him from his home and kids. On the other side, his wife was looking at him with love, not judging him. At this point, I *insist* on knowing which substance kept her afloat. Heroin? Chocolate muffins? Marijuana? She claims it was prayer—tons and tons of unceasing prayer. Plus, yes, a bit of chocolate. Not even her girlfriends gave her any real comfort, because none of them supported a decision so far from the standard, "normal," instinctive route. And especially because Elisabetta had chosen not to complain about it, not even to her closest friends. It's true that we women, once we vent, are already halfway to solving our problems simply by talking them through with someone. But it's also true that complaining can feed resentment, anger, bitterness—the evil inside us. So sure, vent—but in moderation, a little at a time.

I recall a very special woman once asking a girl of my generation (I was still in the "idiotic phase," but with a tendency to sadness, so call it late adolescence), "Which brand are *you*?" The girl looked down at her shirt, thinking maybe she was wearing Lacoste or Polo. (At that point, I was mostly wearing the "hand-me-downs from my older cousin" brand.) But before she could answer, the woman said, "I'm the 'empty' brand. There's an emptiness in me.

When I was your age, I'd often feel it—sometimes it bit and really hurt; other times it just made me sad. Then I realized we fill that emptiness by loving without asking anything in return: when you do something nobody else feels like doing, when you get up and inconvenience yourself, when your Old Self earns nothing from it, when you decide to keep an elderly grandma company."

Elisabetta did exactly that: she allowed herself to be contradicted, to be changed by reality. Saints are those who *do* change, who let the Lord, through circumstances and trials, upend their equilibrium. Often it's money or comfort that keeps us from changing. People don't want to change, don't want healing; they prefer a stable life, even if it's a miserable one.

One of the miracles in Elisabetta's story is that she managed to spare her children too much suffering—emphasis on *too much*, because kids always pick up on everything, whether they realize it consciously or not. But she took away the rancor, showing that one parent was steady, still hopeful. It gave the children a sense of security—they knew someone was steering the ship, that they weren't drifting in chaos, the way kids usually feel when parents separate. If one of the two *remains* in the marriage, that can save them. Even if that person is alone, in pain, and maybe it appears the kids even despise them for "not fighting back." Still, I'm certain no drop of that suffering, endured in order to stay—and to stay with a good heart—goes to waste. *I* would have immediately imagined new uses for my husband's part of the house once I kicked him out and changed the locks. First, I'd move in a three-door wardrobe just for me (not that I'd know what to fill it with, beyond the clothes I once thought were suitable for clubbing—clothes I wouldn't wear again except under torture). As for my husband's clothes, I'd neatly cut them into uniform strips to dry the kitchen floor, though I'd reserve his cashmere sweater for dusting. His sprawling CD collection, meanwhile, would be sold cheap to some junk dealer, ideally a fan of the opposing soccer team. And then I'd expand my kitchen cabinets significantly — because when one door closes, a jar of Nutella opens.

I admire so much those people who, despite stumbles and doubts and tears and wavering, manage not to meet evil with evil. In all painful situations, Christianity offers an alternative, because it's not a doctrine, it's a resemblance. We resemble God when we get treated as He was — when we lose everything; when, facing a reality that makes us suffer, we don't fixate on how we've been wronged, we don't lament that it's all a mess, we don't see the devil lurking in every corner, but we simply trust that these hardships are the chisel God uses to carve us into a masterpiece. But man is a historical being, not a block of stone, and he can do certain things only in certain moments of his life. The moment is given to him to make a leap of faith, because, as the Psalm says, "Man in his prosperity never learns." When God allows suffering, it's so we can become like Him. He wants friendship with us — complete transparency. And what's better than being friends with the Chief of the Universe? So we shouldn't ask to be delivered from the trial but rather that He stays close to us in it, because having Him close is far better than "feeling good." We seek to know what He wants, and He looks after our concerns, like friends do for one another.

Elisabetta chose to resemble God in her powerlessness: God can do anything, but He *cannot* force us to love Him. Likewise, she didn't try to *force* her husband to love her. She respected his freedom, including his freedom to be wrong. (That's precisely what God does with us.) She fought, because it can't have been easy for her; she fought not to accuse him when he came home, knowing full well he'd been with the other woman. She asked him no questions and shared, with gentleness, everything about the kids—whom he also deeply loved.

If we let our capacity to care—our emotional lives—meet God, we turn a corner: if we don't say "I can't," we allow the Spirit to grow in us, gently taking advantage of our emotional side as fertile ground. Then the Spirit gains strength over that Mr. Hyde we each have inside, and we don't know how it happens, but we begin to transform. Living with someone who hates you leaves no middle ground: either you throw him out or you live as a Christian. You have to shine so brightly that the other person's sin is exposed by contrast. Whatever hurt you receive, you don't respond in kind.

She found herself in that scenario—like certain remarkable souls the Lord has chosen—where need becomes vocation: you're starving, and so you have to learn to be a baker. You're starved for love, so you become a sign to others, showing them how to survive when love fails you.

Of course, the path Elisabetta took isn't the *only* one, nor does it mean anyone choosing differently is wrong. I always tell my husband I believe in open relationships: meaning, if he cheats, I'll open him from jugular to belly button like a mussel. (And I suspect *my* reaction would be the more normal, realistically speaking.)

But what she decided is really what every baptized person should aim for: asking God to become the most important person in our lives. So forgiving like Elisabetta did doesn't mean she can "live without her husband's love" but that she's begging God to take that spot. It's the same choice made by a saint who lived "separated under the same roof," and wouldn't you know it, she was also named Elisabetta—Elisabetta Canori Mora. In her case, God answered with a blatant, tangible presence (with miraculous signs). With others, He draws near more discreetly and silently.

As Fr. Antonio Sicari writes, a Christian marriage is a sacrament—a means, a sign of something bigger and deeper: the love of Jesus that embraces both spouses. And because Elisabetta's husband denied that bigger and deeper reality, "the Bridegroom decided to take the place He was entitled to, even physically—through some extraordinary manifestation of His presence. But make no mistake: certain mystical experiences granted to the saints are indeed unique and extraordinary. Yet God gives them to a few so as to manifest what free gift is offered to all.[19] He shows us the ordinary grace found in all sacramental marriages. Every Christian spouse must sooner or later—partly through suffering, partly through joy—learn the distance between creature and Creator."

And here's the loveliest part, which applies to any couple—even if, thankfully, there's no cheating, just the everyday grind or the pain we *all* go through at some point in marriage: noticing that the other's love doesn't always reach us the way we'd hoped. "In a Christian marriage, *everything* is sacrament: the love the two are able to give each other is the shining side; the love a spouse either cannot or will not give becomes the 'virginal' side of the sacrament, the part that points directly to Christ and directly calls upon His presence. Even if only one spouse realizes this, life fills up with mercy—and can also fill with miracles."

For our friend Elisabetta—the non-saintly one—her miracle is that her husband came back and got down on his knees a thousand times to apologize, and now they're together with a brand-new covenant, deeper and more genuine. (Though for me, he's still a jerk. But apparently even jerks can be extremely

---

[19] See *Catechism of the Catholic Church* 2014: "the special graces or extraordinary signs of this mystical life are granted only to some for the sake of manifesting the gratuitous gift given to all."

loved.) In other cases, the spouse never returns and starts up a new relationship, which is a whole other story—those who remain faithful to their marriage even though they're separated, a saga of heroism I may have to write about someday.

Chapter Six

Why Stay Married Even if ...

We Don't Speak the Same Language

I leave the church skirting the walls, trying to appear nonchalant — my usual tactic when I'm completely unpresentable and hoping no one meets my eyes. It's Saturday, I'm not working, and I've thrown on a tracksuit over my nightgown (waking up at 8:57 for 9:00 Mass doesn't do wonders for your wardrobe selection). Even though nobody else can see it, I know I'm on the outskirts of society—one step away from Crocs with socks, if you get my drift. On the other hand, a friend of mine once bought pajamas online, thinking they were a dress; by the time she realized, she still wore them to a wedding, head held high, because it's all about confidence, right?

Of course, if you're hoping no one greets you, you inevitably bump into a dozen acquaintances per square meter: the condo manager from two buildings ago, the secretary from the elementary school of your kid who's now in college. And these folks, summoned from the void, not only say hello but assume you remember their names. Well, they're wrong. I can't help it if everyone's name is so ordinary. If someone was called "that jerk of your aunt's" or "vomit," I'd surely remember. Anyway, among these people dispatched by the universe to punish my hubris (leaving the house without brushing my teeth, hoping to get away with it) is a woman who was the youngest mom at the daycare my last daughters attended. There's a bit of an age gap between us—maybe seven or eight years. She's not named "Ferragni has cellulite," or I'd have remembered, so I do what I always do when I have no clue: I just admit the truth. "Good to see you again, even if you've lost weight and so I should hate you. But I can't recall your name." I'm not sure if that's an invitation to chat, although at this point, my only goal is to get home, eat breakfast, shower, dress, and reenter civilized society.

Daniela—that's her name—replies that yes, she's lost weight, but not on purpose: she's having a marital crisis. If I'm up for a coffee, maybe she'll tell me about it. Leaving aside my urge to punch anyone who slims down from stress, I have trouble saying "no." So we end up sitting near the church at one of the saddest cafés in Europe. Sad in the Roman way—this city can be sublime and squalid practically on the same block, mixing carved capitals with a bidet ditched on the sidewalk.

Daniela starts talking about her husband, and gradually I recall bumping into him a few times at the preschool: he was a good-looking, polite, friendly geologist. She must feel like confiding in me because even back then—though I hadn't yet written any books—I was dishing out unsolicited advice gleaned from my Confessions with Fr. Emidio, who always shared some secret of the male psyche. The truth is, I'd go to Confession with Fr. Emidio mostly to give a quick rundown of my very few sins and then launch into a detailed list of *my husband's* many shortcomings—which in my opinion more than justified my outbursts. Then one day, Fr. Emidio snapped. I won't repeat his exact words (my public image depends on it), but the crucial point is that from then on, he began explaining why I hadn't understood a thing about how men operate. It was a revelation for me and changed a season of my married life. Ever since, I've been happily sharing his insights with others.

One of the lessons that struck me most from that pivotal Confession was that a man thinks he can understand a woman. *Thinks* so, but he can't. Yes, men speak another language, but they believe they can translate "woman" as Italians do Spanish: by winging it. Maybe they don't get every *palabra*,[20] but *más o menos*,[21] they do okay, i.e., *te las cavas*[22] (we figure throwing in some random S-sound Spanishifies everything—*facias de bronzos*,[23] that sort of thing). The drama is that while female language may resemble male language on the surface, it's completely different. It's like Italian vs. Korean: you don't catch a single syllable. And that comparison isn't random. Once, I interviewed a Korean cardinal, and before the translator kicked in, I couldn't tell if he was saying "Life is wonderful, the sun is shining," or "All my friends and relatives up to the ninth degree have died in misery." His face was that impassive. I would have done anything to provoke some emotional response—maybe wave, unbutton my blouse, toss him a Pocket Coffee[24]—but in the end, I chickened out. I was still a RAI[25] journalist, after all. Anyway, I learned their language is notoriously tricky because the meaning of every word depends on the tone used for each syllable—each can have up

[20] Spanish: "word." (The Italian word for "word" is *parola*.)
[21] Spanish: "more or less." Similar to the Italian equivalent, *più o meno*.
[22] Spanish: "you scrape it," similar to the Italian *te la cavi*, "you get by." In the Italian original, this was a pun: "te la cavi, anzi, 'te las cavas.'"
[23] Spanish: "bronze faces." Similar to the Italian, *faccias di bronzo* (literally "bronze face"), which is equivalent to the English expression "poker face."
[24] A chocolate with espresso inside.
[25] Radio Audizioni Italiane, Italy's national public broadcasting company.

to six meanings, which is basically how women's language works too: *it's all about tone.*

For example, a man offers, "Want some help?" because he simply wants to know if you need a hand, and you respond, "Thanks, I'll do it myself."

Okay, let's unroll the sacred scroll and figure out the meaning of those four words. We've established that it's all in the tone. Spoken gently, they can mean: "Thank you, my dearest, but you've already helped me so much. You took the kids to school even though it was my turn. You let me sleep in, and I'm grateful. Now just rest—I think I can handle this. But it made me happy that you asked." Or we can have the sour version: "Right, no thanks, leave it. I always end up doing everything anyway, so clearly you don't care about me. You only hurry around for your mother—you never bother about me. Look, now that I say 'no thanks,' you don't even insist. If you really wanted to help, you'd ask me again, but the second I turn you down, you just wander off. Guess you don't care anymore."

To a man's ear, those two lines sound exactly the same—"Thanks, I'll do it myself"—because he doesn't have the equipment to distinguish tone. He doesn't speak Korean, as it were. There *are* men who can parse it, but typically only during that get-you-into-bed phase—or else they're one of those eerie male specimens who know absolutely everything from poplin vs. canvas to your mother's middle name, and I'd be wary: they're hiding something.

Normal men, if they *do* listen, only catch the literal meaning. "No, thanks," is "No, thanks." They're not suspecting the two possibilities mentioned above, nor the other twenty-seven variations in between—ranging from "You're not capable, whereas I'm strong," to "I wish I could ask for your help, but I'm too proud and hate being a bother. However, if you insisted ...," or the heroic, "It's not fair to ask you to do more, so even though I don't feel like doing it, I'm a heroine (*sigh*, like Scarlett O'Hara), and I can face anything on my own, even if it's crossing Siberia with a stroller, an umbrella, and four toddlers." Or the cunning, "I'll do it myself now so I can ask you later if we can have friends over for dinner."

I know men may feel a hint of despair at the mere sight of this sacred scroll. Don't. Just accept it. Don't even try to translate us—it's impossible. A woman isn't "translatable"; you can only *learn* her.

The catch is, you men can never rest. Especially early in a relationship, if you hear "Thanks, I'll do it myself," you naïvely assume it means precisely that. Your single neuron relaxes, all content, heading for the couch or doing whatever else. You might even be a bit disappointed because, hey, you wanted to help your woman—that's your way of showing care. But you figure there'll be a next time. What you don't know is the internal hurricane your silent exit has unleashed.

The fundamental issue is that a woman wants to be *intuited*. She wants a man to do the right things without her having to ask (which belongs to the imaginary domain known as the Conditional Subjunctive of Unrealism). That is, I'd like my husband to spontaneously realize we need new sheets for the kids, because I can't stand asking ("When do kids outgrow teddy-bear sheets, anyway?"). He should be so delighted to spend time with me that he even offers to accompany me to exchange the feathered sandals I bought in too small a size. (The feather detail dulls all my rational faculties; I'll buy anything, even shoes two sizes too small, because I assume I can somehow morph them from a 40 to a 42 wide.)

Blessed Is the Day We "Got It Wrong"

Daniela lays out a series of similar episodes: she wants to be intuited and then says, "If you haven't figured it out, never mind," while he asks her just to be clear about what she wants.

"The problem is, when I start venting, he listens for the first twenty seconds and then starts proposing solutions and giving advice. He never does the one thing I really want: listen. Understand how hard things are for me, see how much I do, tell me I'm a great mom—the best—his dream wife." But that never happens. Men just can't do it. When you say, "Look at these bags under my eyes," their single neuron forgets it's supposed to reply, "No, you look wonderful, I don't see any bags." Instead, they'll say they don't care, because truly, they don't.

I've watched this movie before—it's a classic. Probably the most basic male-female misunderstanding: a woman wants a man who *listens*, who looks at her like she's beautiful, who understands her weaknesses, exhaustion, insecurities. The man, on the other hand, builds his self-esteem by proving to himself and others that he *can handle* things. Plus, solving problems is how he loves. So when he hears the woman he cares about complaining about some issue, he subconsciously feels accused: "Wait, does this mean I'm not handling things right?" His gut reaction is, "Well, what do you want me to *do*?" And that's where my own rants crash on the rocks. "Nothing. I don't want you to *do* anything. I'm not complaining or blaming you; I'm not asking for advice or help. I just need you to show me empathy, say you recognize my exhaustion isn't from me doing something wrong but from me taking on a thousand wonderful tasks—and by the way, my butt looks fantastic. That's the base line. Just say it, always."

I really think my husband would let himself be killed for me or our kids—he gives his life a bill at a time, one errand run at a time, one grocery trip at a time. Yet I also believe he's enrolled in a course specifically designed to teach him to always, unfailingly, say the most unhelpful thing possible. He's unbelievably good at that. Occasionally he slips up and almost says something comforting, but then he snaps right back on track. I suspect he did a master's program at Yale or some elite school for top-tier husbands.

A typical scenario: I come home from work exhausted. "I'm so tired, I answered two hundred messages, I still have four emails to write and have to drive two daughters around. I need to finish an article and prep dinner. I promised to read a friend's book and write a review. Plus, I really want to say that Marian prayer tonight before 3:00 a.m., and I need some sleep, but I also ..." I go on and on for a few minutes, which is basically a faint buzz to my husband's ears. By the time I get to "messages"—the seventh word in—he's turned off the audio channel. His hearing works on a hashtag principle. The word "pastries," for instance, reactivates him instantly. Typically, I'll say, "Elisabetta wants a divorce because her husband's cheating on her, and do you know how she found out? She noticed he bought ... oh, by the way, I bought pastries." And he's, "Where'd you put them?" So you see, his ears go dead to sentimental drama (mine or anyone else's) or any sensational revelations about my friends, yet they perk up when they hear random key phrases that are meaningless to me. And it's not just food. He really tunes in at words like "Netanyahu," "deep state," "gatekeeper," or "social experiment," plus classics like "Red Brigades,"[26] "Moro,"[27] and "9/11." Conversely, phrases

---

[26] An Italian Marxist-Leninist armed terrorist group active in the 1970s–1988.

[27] Aldo Moro, the former Italian prime minister and the president of the Christian Democracy party (the majority party at the time) was kidnapped and murdered in 1978.

like "I feel," "I'm worried about," or "I'm anxious" all make him flick off his mental radio.

Whenever I complain he doesn't focus on me enough, the conversation goes something like this:

Husband: "It's not true that I don't listen. We spoke for ten minutes this morning."

Me: "That doesn't count. That was about the anti-smog driving ban, who'd take which car, and where to park. That doesn't count as real listening. I want to tell you how I *am*. Come on, Bernardo, you were here—didn't we only talk about logistics? Why are men so closed off?"

Bernardo: "Aw, Mom, if I *have* to talk, I do. Ten minutes total: I tell you my entire life, then spend the other nine on the PlayStation."

If I'm breading chicken cutlets—an activity that defines a large portion of my motherhood—and I ask one of the men in the house to text my friend who's worried about her second child, I dictate something like: "*Hi Francesca, sorry, but I'm in the kitchen with messy hands*"—keeping it vague so she imagines me stuffing a roast quail instead of making more cholesterol bombs—"*I'll call you later once I can, but I just want you to know I'm thinking about you, I love you, and I'm sure your son will find his path in life. All we can do is keep looking at him with that loving gaze that awakens his desire for goodness and beauty, and never stop praying, because God is his Father and Mother before you or anyone else could be. Got it, honey?*" And he's like:

"Sure."

"Wow, you're fast."

"I wrote: 'I'll call you back.'"

So I'm sure Daniela's husband—don't expect me to remember his name as well; I recall his face and his geologist profession, so he'll be "Geo" from now on—does genuinely care about her. But they've hit a phase I'd call the "Spa Phase": not spa as in hot tubs, massages, and white bathrobes, rather, SpA[28]—they serve a purely administrative state of running their life around kids, jobs, mortgage, shuttle service, extracurriculars, groceries, lunches, dinners (all worsened by their living in Rome, a city where traffic is paralyzing and public transport almost nonexistent). They do it all but forget the best part: carving out time to look each other in the eye and *talk*. But I know that to men, the expression "We need to talk" is worse than hearing their wife say, "Is this yours?" while holding up a strange bra she found under the couch.

Anyway, finding time: interrupting "the SpA life" now and then, and not just to talk. Sometimes you can share a moment quietly, without saying anything, yet still look into each other's eyes. You keep your thoughts inside, but you're there, doing some-thing together for the pure enjoyment of it—just to rediscover that whatever was there at the start is still there now. You don't have to be rich—Daniela objects, pointing out that between his researcher's salary and her graphic designer pay, plus two kids and a mortgage, there's hardly money for romantic weekends. But you don't need to go anywhere fancy—just a park is enough, as long as you allow yourself the luxury of doing nothing or, rather, *the courage* to set aside all your to-do's.

Sometimes, in fact, talking is *not* the thing you need. It pains me to say it, but my husband is right (by now he'll have gotten bored with reading, so he'll never know I've agreed with him—he probably couldn't handle the shock). Often, you don't need more talk. Because frequently, what comes out is our "crazy housemate"

---

[28] SpA stands for *Società per Azioni*, which translates to a joint-stock company.

side, that part inside us that "spews nonsense nonstop" (copyright Fr. Emidio). Its main goal is to alienate us from our reality by painting it dull, unfortunate, flawed. Everyone's "inner crazy housemate" sabotages in its own special way: victimhood, envy, pride ... sometimes focusing on the future with grim predictions, sometimes on the past, twisting our memories. When *she's* the one talking, you shouldn't listen.

Daniela isn't a woman of faith, so I can't quite say this directly to her, but the way to cleanse your brain is prayer. Prayer and reading God's Word, replacing our subconscious with a different source of knowledge about ourselves and the world. Trusting Someone Else. Our hearts are an abyss—we are double, triple, ten-layered. The way to unify ourselves when something upsets or hurts us is to go to God and ask Him to show us our true face, revealing His own. "Lord, I am who You make me."

The trouble is, Daniela's far from seeing it that way (maybe not for long, who knows). But the episode she shares resonates with me: she says she felt really hurt yesterday because she had a day off and planned on doing twenty-four thousand things, including some for herself—getting her hair done, grabbing a coffee with a friend, checking out a store that's closing and liquidating, going to Pilates (because sadly, hanging laundry doesn't count as a sport). Then her old friend Guilt chimed in, telling her she needed to invite her husband's sick aunt for dinner—the aunt who's always complaining that nobody wants to be with her and she's all alone, possibly because it's true that nobody wants to be with her (but that's just a hypothesis). Anyone who frequently attempts such suicidal "generosity" (like me) knows that shoehorning a dinner invitation into an already busy day doesn't just occupy dinner—it devours almost everything else. In the end, Daniela had zero free time left for herself. She hoped that if not the aunt, at least her husband would express some gratitude, even minimal—like, say, ninety-nine long-stem roses, a small diamond, maybe an air show by the Italian Frecce Tricolori[29] trailing pink smoke that spells THANK YOU DANIELA. But no. Geo never thought of it because, being male, he just figured, "She invited her, so I guess she *wanted* to." A man can't grasp the mesh of guilt, conditioning, expectations, and hidden motives that sometimes take us hostage. We don't find it straightforward to say, "I don't feel like it, so I won't do it." We do it, and we're actually happy to do it, but we'd love someone to acknowledge how wonderful, fantastic, toned, and flawless we are.

Plus, in this particular case, Geo was tense over a mistake at work and an impending email from his boss. In his internal universe, there wasn't room for other concerns—and certainly not for his wife's exhaustion, given that she was the one who made the dinner plans anyway.

Putting yourself in the other's shoes—seeing how they feel, how they view the problem—can be more daunting than intergalactic travel (and what's worse, you should really do it multiple times per day). It's an artisanal effort requiring a slow, patient conversion process. He has his history and insecurities, maybe more trouble dealing with mistakes. She, on the other hand, is more resilient, having grown up in a family that taught her independence early on. The imprint of our family histories (plus our personal journeys) is huge. Translating each other means factoring that in. It isn't just a matter of words but also the specific weight each event carries for us.

A woman craves *love*; a man craves *respect*. A man feels his wife's criticisms as disrespect, while the woman perceives the man's lack of closeness as lack of love. But both started with good intentions:

---

[29] The aerobatic demonstration division of the Italian Air Force.

the woman criticizes him because she wants him to do better and because she feels unloved; the man steps away to avoid escalating the conflict, and that withdrawal strikes her as further lack of love. She complains and criticizes him even more; he withdraws further, kills the conversation, and the cycle continues. Someone has to break it and change first—and, in my experience, this only happens if we strive for God to be our primary relationship.

So it's on you to begin. Yes, you reading this. The change starts with us. We decide not to listen to the nonsense rattling around in our heads and try to think the other person's way—loving him in a language he understands. I should love my husband by *doing* things (in his case, actually *not doing* certain things: I need to cancel commitments and not force him to meet more people whose names he'll have to learn—he doesn't hate people; they can exist, but just not in his space, okay?). Meanwhile, he should love me with words full of admiration and occasionally bad-mouthing other women—randomly, because you know women hate territorial incursions. It's a control issue.

All this—learning a freer love, one that loves the other in a way he can actually comprehend, without trying to control or own him, expressing it in a language he speaks—is something we can't give ourselves. It happens only if we entrust ourselves to God, above all by praying.

Only God can make that miracle. If a man hands himself completely over to a woman, she'll domesticate him, controlling him to death; but a woman actually needs a man who can stand firm. If a woman hands herself over entirely to a man, he'll dominate her; yet a man needs a woman who snaps him out of his selfishness.

Truly encountering one another in depth is a lifetime's work. Being "one flesh" is the goal, not the starting point, of marriage—and having a good interpreter is the first step.

Chapter Seven

Why Stay Married Even if …

We Don't Share the Same Faith

A friend of mine—whose love life was, to put it mildly, rather eventful—used to say that finding the "right person" out there is impossible. That person could be hidden in any of five continents, and he surely had already passed through the metro station she was stepping off at, just three minutes earlier. So since aiming for "the right person" was impossible, she focused on finding one who was "only slightly wrong." I tried repeatedly to explain that her method—testing out literally everyone—wasn't going to work. You can often tell from a single conversation if someone's completely unhinged.

Eventually, after a long stretch of that phase, she succeeded: she married a man who was "barely" the wrong one. Now, when she and I chat on the phone during my "office hours"—which actually take place in my car (no longer that trash-can-on-wheels Ka, but a Mini perpetually packed with mandarin peels, Coke Zero cans, and scraps of long-forgotten sandwiches)—I tend to play counselor, even though I'm more like the eccentric old aunt. At least I'm no longer trying to talk her into settling down and getting married, the way I used to do with other friends a few years ago. Back then, I had "A Dream Is a Wish Your Heart Makes" and "Gonna Take You There" on repeat in the car stereo, belting out Disney tunes with my daughters and rolling the windows up at traffic lights so nobody would hear me. Nowadays, though, my girls have all passed six feet tall, and I find myself singing, "*Fumo Presidential, no, fra', non resto mai senza*"[30] without realizing, up until yesterday, that I was basically glorifying marijuana. I can only imagine what people thought, hearing a middle-aged mom sounding so scandalously dissolute.

Actually, these days it's my friend Martina—the one who used to be all about having a good time—who's preaching to *me*. In the meantime, the Lord somehow seduced her heart, the way He sometimes does with His more rebellious children. Now she's the one who keeps reminding me of the things I've written (my husband does that, too, for what it's worth—if only I'd known, I might never have published anything!). She's the one saying women need to stop trying to change and control their men. The "new Martina" insists that each of us has to work on our own perspective and our own conversion, not on reforming the people around us.

This wise friend of mine seems to have used up all her "lives," like in a video game: she's made every possible mistake (truly *every* one), and now she's basically the woman I wish I could be. I really should write a book about the issue of envy at some point, if I weren't so embarrassed about it. Martina let God heal her. She allowed Him to mend her relationships and forgave not only her parents—and, more importantly, asked *their* forgiveness—but also her siblings and her girlfriends; she's a wife and mother who has given her heart back to God. Not *fully*, otherwise she'd be the Blessed Virgin, but you know, she's made a decisive surrender.

[30] Beginning lines of the Italian rap song "Presidential" by Gemitaiz, featuring Rome Fortune. The verse she's singing means, "Presidential Smoke, no, bro, I never run out."

She's learned a new way of loving: free from possessiveness, living in freedom, no longer viewing people as disposable objects. By living out her relationship with God, she rediscovered her own greatness, dignity, and uniqueness; from there, she learned a new way to be present for the people she cares about. With God, she rebuilt her heart: she stopped being the coy "girly-girl" caught up in seduction and jealousy, and she put down her weapons of rivalry with other women—because, as she says, "Christ is the ultimate psychologist," and now she cares only about *His* opinion of things.

"There's just one area where I can't help hoping my husband changes," she says, "rather than choosing to love him exactly as he is. It's that he's so distant from the Church. I just can't bring myself to accept that. Not because I think I'm better than him, or that I don't believe in God's infinite mercy, but because I'm certain we can't be truly happy and truly fruitful—can't bear real, abundant fruit—outside the Church." (Told you she's a changed woman: these days not even the average parishioner—let alone some priests—tend to believe something like this anymore.) "I know it's not remotely 'ecumenical' to say so. But I can say it because I'm not a bigot. I've been there, *outside* the Church. I lived there for a long time. I savored all the so-called 'freedoms' (which were actually just slavery), and I know that nothing can make you truly happy deep inside when you're cut off from the sacraments. But God is an ocean of delight, and the enemy doesn't want us to know it. I love Luca with all I have—so how can I accept that my husband is settling for something less in life, that he might never encounter the One who fills the heart, who truly brings every talent to bloom, levels the mountains, fills the valleys?" (Yes, she occasionally sounds as if Isaiah the prophet has possessed her, but that's better than when she used to channel Lady Gaga.)

Blessed Is the Day We "Got It Wrong"

I get that this issue might seem minor compared to the typical problems couples face—it's pretty rare to divorce over something like that, and the Catholic Faith isn't exactly fundamentalist. Still, a lot more people than you'd think suffer because one spouse is far from faith. For a believer whose relationship with God is the core of everything, it *hurts* when the other person is indifferent to that. And it can be a real problem because that stance affects countless choices—from foundational couple decisions like openness to life and money matters (two very concrete, crucial flashpoints) to how you face any challenge and how you raise your children. Above all, there's the sadness of not sharing the most important thing of all, not being fully one in the deepest part of your life.

"Maybe I *shouldn't* have married someone who doesn't share my faith," Martina says in one of her "Judgment Day" moments during which she regularly questions her entire life.

Well, first off, you're on a diet—and we know perfectly well that by day five, you're so hungry you're about to feel sentimental toward the honey in your hair mask, which means you're definitely not being objective. I don't trust you right now. Plus, any sentence starting with "I should (or shouldn't) have ..." belongs on Radio Satan—yes, the one that's always buzzing away in our subconscious, trying to make us hate our life. The devil is like a scorpion waving its tail right in front of our eyes, forcing us to stare at the past and injecting us with that venom: what could have been supposedly surpasses what we have now. In reality, the secret is to do exactly the opposite: embrace what we *do* have as the only place where we can truly live and encounter real life. And finally, even if hypothetically you *did* "make a mistake," it doesn't matter anyway—indeed, Martina, every married person thinks that at least once (some are more than just grazed by the thought, and more than once). In fact, *blessed* is the day we got it wrong, because this is precisely our path to salvation, our path of conversion. This is your story—do your best in it, period.

I read somewhere on the internet: "Everyone complains about Monday, but it's not like Tuesday is some Rio Carnival." Meanwhile, we should greet each Monday as one more gift granted us. We're always running from reality because it's going badly—really badly—but we miss that it's crafted for a *meeting* with God's eternal love. If we want to live, we must embrace the plan God wrote into our reality (as opposed to our so-called "self-determination," which is probably what caused all the chaos in our life to start with, if you recall).

Anyway, what if your husband seems not to believe in God? I see why that pains you, but we don't know the blueprint for his life. Maybe it's all part of a plan—maybe it's meant to test and strengthen your faith, keep you on your knees. If a good and genuine desire doesn't come to pass, it's probably for a greater good. But if St. Teresa of Ávila says prayers for someone's conversion *cannot* go unanswered, I believe her. In the early years of my own marriage, my husband never went to Mass, not even on Sundays. Now he's further along in faith than I am—God is creative and way more imaginative than we are, but it takes some time and a lot of prayer. There was a time when I fancied myself a missionary who was going to save the entire world. In reality, I was just a nobody who couldn't even convince herself in the mirror. One day, I found a little prayer card of Don Bosco lying on the ground (in Rome you can find anything on the ground: bathtubs, money, wild boar, rosaries). On the back, it said roughly: "I have never thought of anything except doing my duty, praying, and trusting Our Lady." (I'm quoting from memory, because I ended up gifting that card to one of my children when he went away for a

year—naturally, he lost it in eight nanoseconds. Who knows if it
slipped out or he used it as a gum wrapper or Kleenex.)

It felt like Heaven was showing me a sign in big letters: *This is
not your business. Do your part, but I love your husband even more than
you do. Don't worry; pray for him.* Obviously, I did more than just
that. I also bugged him, preached at him, tried dragging him to
catechism classes and all sorts of retreats featuring weird folks with
fanny packs who claimed to chat with the Virgin Mary—stuff that
did *not* help my missionary zeal. Indeed, during those meetings,
he'd hiss, "Where the heck have you dragged me?" (and "heck"
wasn't the actual word he used). But in some way, I also managed
to stay in my lane and pray for him. Then the Lord did what He
wanted, in His own time and in His own way, and now I no longer
feel I have to "convert" my husband. If anything, it's the other
way around. He's one of the few people I'll allow to correct me,
even if I don't admit it to him (and he won't see this anyway). I
respect his way of living the Faith, which is more rational, more
sober, less sentimental than mine.

Freedom is always personal. We can *hope* someone meets God,
pray for it to happen, and encourage them if the chance arises, but
we can't make it happen. (In other words, loosen your grip. That's
where I keep stumbling.) The only thing we can do is make our
own faith as genuine and believable as possible. Sometimes we're
monstrous and don't convince anyone. But we have to choose
Jesus Christ, become Him: everything else is just "the pedagogy
of the law," which is a starting point, sure, but eventually it has
to make us *like* Him. We should never forget that. We need to
move beyond mere religion (Christianity looks like a religion, but
it isn't) and enter into a living relationship.

You, Martina, needed that initial strictness to find your footing
after you spent years as a loose cannon begging for identity and

validation—even from lampposts. Like you say yourself, you had "a lot of right moments with all the wrong men." Now, though, lay off the bigotry (I hope you're not offended: Fr. Emidio used to say the same thing to me when I wanted to reshape the world with a flurry of novenas). I'm worried you're one step away from wearing mid-calf skirts and nude pantyhose, but you don't really have to bounce from micro-shorts and halter tops to *that*. You can just dress like normal people, you know?

And oh, the messes you made really were epic. Remember that guy who showed up in Crete when you were vacationing with your girlfriends? You forced him to break up with his long-term fiancée, but meanwhile you'd changed your mind about him yourself, and everything was booked solid so you couldn't leave the island that night. So he slept on a park bench in the yard because *you* were in the house with some German guy with a six-pack who was so incredible in bed that you wouldn't let go of him for a second. Pity that once you got back home, you couldn't even remember his name, so we always called him "Pretty Hair." Or that time you snatched your classmate's boyfriend, thereby violating Article 1 of the "Girlfriend Code," which says, "Your friend's boyfriend is dead to you. If she only sort of likes him, he's in a coma" (he might wake up only if she starts dating someone else, and only after three months). Then you discovered that God doesn't forbid things because He's mean, He points out good and evil to give you something greater. So you started seeking that greater good, gradually noticing that other people exist. You no longer needed to chase approval and affection from everyone, because Someone had satisfied your hunger.

The Kingdom of God is realizing that God is our Father and we're His children, but we have to slowly learn how to spend time with Him—that is, with His children. Often He doesn't expect grand gestures from us. Sometimes just a small 007-like operation can change someone's life—and it isn't even all that hard. He usually doesn't demand heroism; He wants us to be His instruments. The example of love He gives is the Good Samaritan—someone not asked to upend his whole life, but just to pick up the wounded man, bring him to an inn, leave money, and move on. Doing that precise, targeted good is worth more than a thousand sacrifices. That's why truly loving requires intelligence.

We can't change anyone—least of all our spouse. I totally get that it's painful not to share your spiritual journey with him, to withhold that most precious, intimate part of your heart. I've been there myself for a while. Yet in the face of someone else's freedom, we can only step aside. Christ promises fullness and salvation, but not everyone actually wants them.

We *can*, however, be convincing Christians. God has you, Martina, to act on His behalf. He has us. We can look after those people He especially cares about—often the ones we'd sooner stick to the wall with duct tape. Our life of faith, our life in general, shifts gears once we start taking responsibility for whatever was lost. By grace, we line up with God's will and change our plans to serve it. And that's what really challenges those around us: they see us losing something that's ours, enduring other people's messes. It's the only way we can touch hearts, become partners with God.

So when someone provokes or offends you, don't retaliate—remember they're a sibling in need of salvation (yes, that includes your coworkers). You have to put up with other people's issues. All of us suffer from warped reactions, questionable choices, habits, horrifying or senseless thoughts that we'd never dare speak out loud. If a curtain were lifted on our hearts, we'd see we're all a bit off our rockers at times. The biggest temptation is rejecting reality—technology often worsens mental issues, though that's another topic.

Behind every complaint is someone who doesn't want to be where they are. Yet what's asked of us is to surrender to our story, even when we don't understand it. Truly, a lot of things are inexplicable, chaos abounds, and sometimes *we're* not exactly stable either. Your "sober new Martina" persona, for instance, isn't always perfectly sane. Your perfectionism with your kids can be scary. Learn from me—I never bothered berating myself just because the teacher found out I wasn't bathing or feeding my kids in the morning (I was too sleepy). Nor did I do anything drastic when Tommaso, back in elementary school, told his class he wished he were Irish so he could get drunk before sunset. You *can* have imperfect children and still be a good mother. Remember, you might never have gotten such a gift to begin with—you're a walking miracle.

The Lord is gracious, and He's so patient with us at first. Then once you shift gears, you speed up—at least, that's what Fr. Emidio would say. At that point, God wants us to care for others, to reach those who need us. We have to figure out how to proceed, how to do those small, thoughtful gestures for the people He wants to pull back in—He won't do it *without* us. He asks us to jump in quickly so He can then do what He needs to do.

Have patience with your husband. He's the first one on whom you need to practice the gospel. Turn the other cheek, forgive seventy times seven, give your tunic on top of your coat—meaning your time, your tastes, your preferences, your plans. Don't get angry with him; anger just punishes *you* for someone else's misdeeds. You're still working on yourself, still doing your "software update" to the new Martina by replacing your impulsive, reflexive thoughts with God's Word. Stay the course and be patient with him. More importantly, watch out for your own risks along the path of faith, the stumbling blocks to your conversion. Keep these examples in mind (this list isn't originally mine, but I can't remember who said it):

1. *Jesus in the desert:* After you convert, the Lord leads you into the desert so you can get to know your own heart. If He brought you straight into fertile land, you wouldn't be able to handle it. Our adult life often feels like a desert—the grind of the daily routine, eating the same meal over and over, or the "thrilling" mission of going to the hardware store or picking out a new sofa—but it is what we are called to in this moment so we can grow to perfection.

2. *Peter, who, looking at his feet as he walked on water, stopped:* Looking at our own weakness paralyzes us. Sometimes we project that weakness onto others, and everyone suddenly seems terrible. The suicidal person sees reality all too clearly but looks at faith without faith's understanding.

3. *The rich young man who couldn't change because there were things he wouldn't let go of:* It's not just money; it can be our fixations, our grudges, or our certainty that we're right (ahem) and better than others.

4. *Nicodemus, who didn't want to be born anew from above:* When we refuse to abandon our way of understanding reality, we can't reboot ourselves to align with God's Word.

So it always comes back to the same point, whether it's raising kids or converting your spouse: we must work on *our own* conversion first. The only advice I can give you is this: if a woman is sincerely seeking God, sooner or later her husband will follow (even if it's *much* later). If you don't see results, don't assume it's because you're not "good" enough. Some husbands get it only after their wife's death (even a saintly wife like Elisabetta Canori Mora), and some not until their own deathbed. Sometimes, "results," if we can call them that, never appear at all. But it doesn't matter. We have no idea why that is, or what happens in people's hearts secretly. For some wives, a husband who's distant from faith might be the thorn in their flesh (like St. Paul's) that keeps them clinging to God.

One last important thing, Martina: your communion with your husband has to come before everything else. I've seen people put their marriages on the rocks—sometimes outright wrecking them—by running to church to set up chairs for some "star priest's" talk or bouncing constantly from one spiritual group to another in an insatiable "spiritual gluttony." They were forever chasing something new to taste instead of accepting that sometimes it's desert-time—with the same manna each day. Our vocation is to be wives, and *that's* where it all plays out: communion with your husband, which might occasionally mean just watching a movie together—minus reciting the Rosary in your head while staring at the top-right corner of the screen. You have to be fully present, because in that moment, loving your spouse is the most important prayer there is.

Remember another blessed woman with an atheist husband, Élisabeth Leseur. She would go out at night, all stylish and bejeweled, to frequent high-society salons on the Left Bank just to be with him. In the mornings, she volunteered at orphanages, giving away whatever she could—though not the gifts from her husband, whom she tried to love as Jesus loved him, with a gaze full of forgiveness, a gaze that sees into the future, because God always sees us in our future state; He sees us already holy, in the fullness we'll achieve only in Heaven. In His view, time doesn't exist.

Chapter Eight

Why Stay Married Even if ...

Our Children Seem Like a Challenge to Our Bond

"A year before my parents split up," a friend once told me, "I would eavesdrop every evening on their endless arguments downstairs. When I went to bed, their fights would start: my mom did nothing but accuse my dad, and he never answered her. I just wanted them to stop. I would have given anything—maybe gone downstairs and taken all the blame myself—but they never ended. That's why I came to school (we were classmates in high school, remember?) half asleep. I couldn't keep my eyes open."

Yes, I remember, and only thanks to those stories did I figure out how it happened that, after a stellar sophomore year, Filippo suddenly became the worst student in the class.

"I thought it'd be easy to get them to stop fighting, and I couldn't understand why none of the grown-ups did anything to try. The summer before I started my junior year, my parents told me and my brother they were divorcing. In spite of all the arguments, it felt like the ground fell out from under my feet. I had friends whose parents were divorced: they were failures at school and life in general; they were inconsistent with their affections. The events that followed confirmed my fears: my own life got turned upside down. Because once love is gone, telling yourself you're the child of a 'greater love' doesn't help the emptiness inside. I kept doing badly at school, and my mother lost it: she began yelling, cursing, and speaking horribly of my father. The more she did that, the more I stayed out, obviously not studying. My father, too, pulled away from her for good. That's when the new woman showed up, cheerful, upbeat, sunny, beautiful. You could sense the physical attraction between them. Whenever we went out to dinner, it was tangible. Then I'd go back to that house where everything had frozen in time since the separation. Nobody dared sit in Dad's old armchair, and Mom would lash out at me because going out with Dad and 'that woman,' in her eyes, meant I'd taken their side. Her blowups grew more frequent and longer, and there was no one to keep her in check, neither my little brother nor me — and because I was the older one, I became the 'man of the house' way too soon. My only weapon was screaming curses louder than she did, but everything fell apart — home life, school, my relationships, all of it. Deep down, I felt I deserved all that misery, as if it was somehow my fault. Maybe that's where the insecurity of kids with divorced parents comes from. I wasn't enough to keep them together. And I hadn't done enough. Things didn't improve even in college: it took me ten years to finish engineering school, while my father was happy, had more kids, and supported both us and his new family financially. Meanwhile, my mom became more and more unhinged, and my brother and I were still the only ones looking after her. I don't know by what grace I kept my faith. In my worst despair, riding around on my scooter, I'd often end up at Monteluce and slip into the Poor Clares' church to pray, or sometimes I'd go to early-morning Mass before school or in those interminable college years. Sure, during sleepless nights spent mindlessly flipping channels, I might stop on some porn now and then, but I never cut that thread with God — even though I cursed Him a lot. In those days, the Church's uncompromising stance on marriage was a critical anchor for me, sometimes my only one. And thanks to so many good priests, I always felt welcomed and understood by the Church. The Church still loves sinners, but that clarity was a relief to me: there was a real, solid reason for my pain. Nowadays, confusion seems in style and we try to go easy on the guilty, but back then, the Church's straight talk helped me name my suffering. I've forgiven my parents, but the scars remain and always will. I've carried enormous burdens, and I tried not to let a single ounce fall on my wife or kids — though sometimes, seeing the problems they face, I panic and think I haven't succeeded. As if the sentence that landed on me were a 'life with no parole.'"

I've told him many times that even though I know how much he's suffered, he wouldn't be the wonderful person he is today if he hadn't lived that story. He wouldn't be such a loyal and kind husband — even though his wife is difficult, despite the fact that he is an attractive man (in high school, I never saw it, but he's grown better-looking with age, something that apparently happens to some men and to zero women, alas). He's also an extraordinary father who's been through suffering as a son, which makes him uniquely supportive of his own children. Maybe he's managed to take that "life sentence" and make it fruitful — but we have to admit, very few people can do the same.

Children, first and foremost, are a powerful reason to stay together. I know, we're not supposed to say that, because our culture is steeped in the refrain "You can't stay together *only* for the kids," not to mention the other gem: "Better to divorce than to fight constantly." It's a line screenwriters feed us, and it's what parents who can't handle it anymore understandably tell themselves with a heavy heart.

But let me flip the perspective. Even if it's hard and you fight a lot, no amount of fighting is worse than divorce. If your children's

Blessed Is the Day We "Got It Wrong"

well-being is at stake, you have to do everything in your power to stay. Yes, it's tough, and harder in some cases than others, but it can be done—even though at times it might feel like the spouses are dying by deciding to remain together. But at least the kids can see you're *trying*. By contrast, if a child knows he's formed from the flesh of a man and a woman who abandon each other, it causes a pain that can unravel his very identity. I doubt anyone—not me—really comprehends the depth of a child's suffering, how irreparably alone he feels when it dawns on him that not even for his parents—whose love, up to a certain age, he assumed was unconditional—does he matter more than anything else in the world. We can't grow up without the assurance that we're everything to someone. (Later in life, we discover only God can love us like that, but as kids, it's the parents who provide that sense of security.) Sure, we grow up, move on, but the scar remains even into adulthood. I know dozens of men and women in my circle of friends who still carry sadness years later—unless they've met a Father bigger than anything, and even *He* can't make everything disappear.

Between our happiness and our children's, *theirs* must come first (assuming what we think we're "giving up" is real happiness in the first place). If a child can handle the pain of a divorce, why can't you, as an adult, handle the pain of a (supposed) emotional loss? Why can't you give up that other man or other woman? With an exception for violence—where separating is vital, both for safety and because it might shock the abuser into recognition (the Church says this as well)—in all other cases, you have to try to the bitter end. I have lots of friends like Filippo, grown men who've been fundamentally shaped by that parental split. Some ended up divorcing their spouses themselves; others live in constant fear of being abandoned or failing to love forever; still others suffer from relationship dependencies—women who "loved too much," men

132

who constantly guarded themselves from being duped. A few (very few) have become special people but deeply wounded—just like my friend Filippo, who's one of the best human beings I know, but who paid a huge price. I've said it before and I'll say it again: for little ones, it's devastating to sense that no one loves them more than *everything*—more than themselves. Yet that's exactly what each heart craves: absolute love. Our job is to come as close to that need as we can for our children. Yes, we'll love them imperfectly, with limitations, dents, and mistakes, and we'll inevitably hurt them sometimes, blurting out words that wound. But at least we can look them in the eye and say, "I gave it my all. I'm a sinner, half-crazy, hurting in my own ways, but I've done all I could for you. Any time it was possible, I was there for you. You're flesh of our flesh, and for your sake, I'm still learning to love this other person so different and distant from me."

I'll also add, friend who's tempted by divorce, that if right now it seems you're sacrificing everything for them—staying in a marriage "just" because you love your children more than your-self—you may one day find it was the best thing for *you* too. Our hearts are a mystery; we have no idea what life has in store if we decide to climb a mountain that looks too steep and painful. Maybe, past that crag, you'll find a lush valley—an unexpected spectacle. A love that's reborn, restarts, transforms. We should always mistrust ourselves and obey. Above all, mistrust the voice of the enemy murmuring about your life like it's a dark, hope-less cage. There are treasures "no eye has seen nor ear heard" prepared for us.

But there's another angle to this: beyond being a huge reason not to split, children can also be a source of division in a couple. First, because when we become moms, we risk turning *completely* into "mothers," forgetting we're above all wives. I say this in my seductive "writing attire"—a teddy-bear robe, thick glasses because "who's going to see me," callused feet with the chipped remains of some prehistoric pedicure. My underwear situation isn't much better: since our twins graduated from the granny-panties at Walmart to Victoria's Secret, I'm left wearing whatever they toss out. The transformation from a girl who changes sixteen times before going out to a woman who grabs the softest rag that falls out of the closet (because she just can't cope with a button that's a bit tight—and it's clearly the button's fault for body-shaming) often reflects the temptation to place all our emotional hopes on our children. Yet the father's role is vital. Whenever someone grows up weird, it's almost always because a father was missing.

That out-of-whack love is a major mistake, especially for the children. They can end up feeling obligated to fulfill our expectations, never quite free to disappoint us—or at least some of them do. Often firstborns have more freedom: they arrived before everyone else, so it's the others who have to battle for room. But for kids, it's incredibly healthy to see that Mom and Dad meet each other's emotional needs. The kids shouldn't have to act as our spouse or therapist; they're not there to console or support us. At least until they're adults, kids aren't responsible for making their parents happy—that's just between the man and the woman (and not even entirely, because ultimately each person is responsible for themselves). For instance, I know I'll never bring my husband that same glow he gets if Roma goes undefeated for six weeks (which happened once); for him, I'll never be as captivating as Dybala,[31] but I can try to come close.

And here I reluctantly admit my friend Marisa is right: whenever I call to gripe about my husband—his gruffness, his minimal

---

[31] Paulo Dybala, an Argentinian football player.

conversation (one day he says he'll write his memoir, five pages max, maybe ten with pictures)—and also complain about how he parents the kids (complaining is my core business, along with laundry), she always reminds me that communion between the parents is the first and most important education for children. It's better to give an occasionally "off" rule, or shaky guidelines, but to do it as a united front, than to be divided. For the kids, standing before "a couple"—two different people who, for love, try to become one—is more precious than any parenting principle. Loving and honoring the father, loving and sheltering the mother, are the best lessons.

In that sense, one more slip-up to avoid is complaining or badmouthing your spouse to the kids. It hurts them, forcing them into an awkward spot: either they bond with the parent who's venting, or they stay silent (but still hear things they shouldn't), or they feel pressured to defend the other. There's also a more subtle, potentially worse method: ridiculing your spouse (often the husband, because many of us are, sadly, quite good at it). It only takes two seconds—a sarcastic comment, a change of tone, an arched eyebrow making the kids feel complicit. It's toxic, and it wounds your children more than you realize.

Sure, some mother-child bond that excludes the father is partly justified by the close relationship formed from birth. Mom translates and interprets every expression and cry; she wakes up at night a minute before the baby wails, and by the time Dad's remembered who that pint-sized person rousing him from sleep might be, Mom has already figured out it's teething pain, not colic. That's fine. In those early years, the bond is normal, governed by hormones. But when the baby is twenty-five, off in Texas, and doesn't respond to messages for an hour, and the (aging) mother (me) is on the verge of calling the Italian embassy in Washington—*that's* when we drift into psychiatric territory. The father has to cut the cord, and the mother has to let him.

In any case, the answer is the alliance between parents. If raising kids means pointing them toward the conversion from "old self" to "new self," from a heart of stone to a heart of flesh, from being self-centered to learning how to love, then parental unity is the greatest, most valuable education we can give them. The parents need to work on presenting a united front on each problem, then show the child that unity—no matter how costly or painful it is behind the scenes.

Take my anxiety, which is a *tiny* challenge when our kids leave the nest. Actually, to say I get anxious is an understatement—I become possessed by it. It's not some pose; it's physical, beyond my control. If they're home late or don't text me, I feel real bodily pain: I can't lift my feet, my stomach clenches, I can't breathe. Killing myself to end the worry is no help (if I die, how can I keep vigil by the door?), so after much suffering, my strategy is to mistrust myself. I've decided to outsource my worrying to my husband. In other words, "I'll only worry if and when you authorize me to." The problem is that my husband never worries. *Ever.*

"So your daughter (when she does something dumb, she's your daughter; when she's brilliant, she's mine) won't pick up the phone? How do you explain it? Either: 1. She's dead. 2. They've chopped off her hands, and now she's wandering around Traste-vere[32] bleeding out, looking for her mom. Or 3. She's dead." (I have to admit, in the thick of panic, sobbing through my dire theories, seeing my husband calmly peeling a pear with total focus or sanding the wall unmoved by my meltdown weirdly soothes me.)

---

[32] A neighborhood in Rome.

Once, it was our son not answering his phone up in Milan. By attempt number 120, at 4 a.m., I shook my peacefully snoring husband awake ("He's probably out of range," were his last words before crashing in thirteen seconds). I announced I was heading out to prowl the outskirts of San Siro in my car to recover the body. In reality, the "body" was napping at a friend's place (my husband had the friend's number but refused to give it to me), and the phone was out of service. So his version was correct. Ever since, I've decided to trust him more than my stomach on matters of worry. I switch off my brain. I look at my stable, unflappable, unwavering husband and try to think as little as possible.

There's a maternal code and a paternal code for raising kids, and it's vital that we authorize each other to use them. The mom has to trust the dad when it's time to cut the cord; the dad has to trust the mom when she senses what's up with this mystery being called a child. Either way, you have to back each other up once you settle on a decision. Once again, *communion* is the key. Get out of the house, go have dinner somewhere or even just share a snack on a park bench—anywhere free from eavesdropping. Look each other in the eye and work out a unified approach.

We know the theory: Mom teaches them how to live, Dad teaches them how to die. Mom is a big "yes"; Dad is a clear "no." Mom helps them say yes to life; Dad helps them accept limits, reality. Mom hands the child over to Dad, telling him that Dad *can* handle it, that she trusts him; Dad teaches the kids to appreciate their mom, telling her she's beautiful. The parents honor and respect each other, allowing each to do their part.

Oh, how wonderful I sound. Fantastic. I know everything. The trouble is that in real life, in real families, things aren't so simple. Many moms are quite happy to have Dad be the authority figure, while Dad withdraws (maybe because we moms want to use him as the "bad cop," to set the rules we choose). So theory's one thing, each family's story is another. The wounds and struggles of each parent are theirs alone, and I hope I'm not laying a heavy burden on anyone's shoulders—an impossible model to replicate, especially since we ourselves are fighting to achieve it. Even more so now that we're midway through the educational crossing: it's too late to turn back (you can't dump them at a highway rest stop; they already know their way home), and the far shore always seems just one stroke away. The teenage years aren't quite over yet, and sometimes I fear I might die before they do, so endless are they.

I get a voice message from a priest, and I unwisely play it even though my son Bernardo is somewhere around. (I thought, *What could Fr. Francesco possibly say that my cordial boy shouldn't hear?*)

"Would you come do a talk at our parish on the topic of kids and parenting?"

Too late—Bernardo has overheard from the next room.

"If you pay me well, I *won't* come say how badly you raised your kids," he bargains.

"But you're my kid too," I reply.

"Yeah, and I turned out fine because I'm self-taught."

Our children (who always know more than we suspect) love to stoke my performance anxiety as a mother—an old hobby. They've been doing it since they were small, like the time one emerged from the bathroom naked, with a towel as a turban, another towel as a cape, and sunglasses, declaring: "My family gave me severe mental problems, I hate everyone around me." He was three. So I'm not exactly brimming with advice, but I can share a few anchor points I cling to whenever I doubt myself (which is basically always).

First off, and most crucially: our kids belong more to God than to us. God loves them more than we do, more than I do, even if that seems impossible. But His heart is bigger, so it holds more love. He knows why He gave *this* child, with these traits, this story, to each couple. Maybe that child struggles with a father who's too strict or too inert, or needs a mother who's not overly clingy, or has to deal with a super-competitive sibling, or an overbearing brother. Every child has their own battle, their own journey. Each of them carries a particular capital sin they'll have to fight. I can't share my own kids' specifics, because they'd sue me; I can only say at some point, parents have to stand on the sidelines cheering with all their hearts—a heart filled with this certainty: our kids are God's, and He made and is making their story, so it leads to good. Some things He *allows*, others He directly *arranges*, but in any case, He knows how to bring good out of everything.

Consider Don Bosco: he lost his father at age two, and that absence seemed to dog him from childhood on. First, his much older stepbrother blocked him from going to school, insisting he work the fields. Then, a priest took him in, let him study (which little Giovanni yearned for), finally treating him like a kind father—and that priest died suddenly. Later, everyone who tried to step into his life with a paternal, kindly manner was taken from him somehow. Yet—maybe *because* of that—Don Bosco became one of the greatest, most fruitful educators and fathers anywhere: he took in thousands of boys in Piedmont and ended up with countless followers who, in turn, became father figures the world over. His vocation grew exactly out of that painful lack. We need to trust that God will bring good out of our own shortcomings and flaws, even for our kids, because everything works for the good of those who love Him—if we ask.

Thus, the most powerful parenting move we can make is to pray for our children, handing them over to a Providence that knows and sees everything and still respects their freedom (just as He does ours). We need to *convince* Him we want His intervention, because the Lord is a gentleman who tiptoes into our lives only if we let Him. Even Jesus asked those who approached Him for healing, "What do you want me to do for you?" He asks us the same question now, while we anguish over our children's hearts, paralyzed by this or that. We'd love to step in for them, suffer in their place, but we can only do one thing, the single most important thing: pray. Pray without ceasing, pray in every moment. Praying matters more than all the other things we do for them, even though we do a lot (and I assume all parents do). Ever since I became a mother, my every action has changed—everything is for them. Every commitment accepted or declined, every purchase, every decision, every move I make is no longer that of a lone individual, but that of a mother. Sure, I do some things for myself, but I do them in a new way, always considering that they exist (like when I go running after everyone's asleep, foolishly hoping they still need a mom around).

Yet sometimes I don't invest enough in what's most essential: prayer. It's more pressing than cooking lunch, running errands, scheduling teacher conferences. (Yes, I'm that keener mom who always goes to teacher conferences; I'll probably try to set up meetings with the CEOs of whatever companies they work for in the future, basket of snacks in tow, because if I'm not there, who's going to check if they're wearing a warm enough sweater?)

In a way, I can fall into anxious praying, just like anxious teacher-meetings, dishing out tips to God. Then again, James and John's mother also tried to pull strings for her sons. But at the core of every prayer is "Your will be done." The one prayer God "must" hear is for our kids' salvation. If we beg God for them to meet Him, confidently believing He'll listen, He can't *not* grant it. He won't fail to give them many opportunities to find Him. And that leads us to the heart of the matter: passing on the Faith. How do we do it? We hope we've sown something. I had my doubts just the other day, though, when one daughter studying St. Augustine yelled from her room: "Ma! Seriously, he thought 'if a man doubts, it means he exists'? So this guy *earned a living* by spouting nonsense like that?"

"Well, he didn't exactly 'earn a living' by thinking ..."

"Oh come on, he must've been *high* all the time!"

Faith could fill not just a book but an encyclopedia, which I wish someone else would write. The little I know is that obviously you can't force faith (past a certain age) or teach it like a subject. You can only *witness* to it. If kids see that their parents treasure their faith above all, it'll challenge them. But they must see two things: it has to be *worthwhile* and it has to be *consistent*.

Worthwhile means a good life, first of all. Fr. Ugo Borghello says that a teen who sees his parents laugh together is safe. Even if once, Lavinia saw a statue of St. Rita and asked, "If I pway a wot, will I get thornies in my head like St. Weeta?" we still try to show we have a life that's appealing.

Consistency, well, that's a real battle. In my view, it's impossible to be genuinely consistent with our faith, but that shifts the front lines. The kids themselves aren't "the problem"; we're not trying to *convert* them. We have to fight our own spiritual fight so that maybe they'll want something similar. ("Mom, don't work in the evenings. If you're in the other room praying, I feel protected," one daughter said back in the days she was still adorable and didn't wipe my kisses off with the back of her hand.)

Then there's the big question of finding a faith community. After a certain age, peers matter far more than family. I envy parents whose kids land in a good youth faith group; ours didn't, and I know that not being plugged into a parish circle is a big "minus" for them. But, oh well. The ideal images of how life "should" be aren't always realistic or from God. True radicality lies in *accepting each day* the poverty of whatever God does—or doesn't—show us. So we keep praying that He provides them with positive situations, a circle of people who can walk with them in searching for Him.

And now, as I carry on—hopefully on the day I keel over I'll breathe a sigh of relief that "the kids weren't too catastrophic" (I've gradually lowered my expectations from raising perfect kids to simply "the least worst outcome")—I'll list some other random observations I've picked up along the way:

1. *Raising children is about proclaiming that life is worth living,* that there is goodness and beauty out there.

2. *You have to love them for free* (even if they're messy, mean, and nasty); love them *mysteriously* (we don't truly know them); love them with your mind, with intelligence, and with hope—seeing who they can become. But it's not enough simply to love them; that love has to reach them, just as in marriage. And love reaches them when you speak each child's language—maybe through gifts, maybe physical affection, words, special time, little acts of service (as that *Five Love Languages*[33] book says). It's a custom job, which can be tough when they're pushing all your buttons. But never stoop to their level in conflicts: remember they're testing your convictions to see if they're cardboard or solid. Look kindly even at their angry outbursts—like kicking you with steel-toed boots.

[33] *The Five Love Languages: How to Express Heartfelt Commitment to Your Mate* by Gary Chapman.

3. *A woman is built to be a mother*, so loving children feels natural, symbiotic. Meanwhile, the father represents *otherness*, especially for daughters, who seek his approval. If he's absent, a girl will look for validation her whole life. If he's present but firm, he educates her well.

4. *Raising them means acknowledging that, yes, life is worthwhile (Point 1), yet the cross exists.* We have to resist the temptation to solve all their problems, remove all obstacles, spare them every hardship — and if anyone deserves the Miss Don't Make Me Laugh sash, it's me, because even if I'm sick with a fever, I'll jump up if my daughter needs not just antibiotics but maybe the all-important item of face powder, because she can't be bothered to go buy it. My energetic offspring have been trying for years to move objects by telekinesis from the couch — gaming controllers, Coke cans, bags of chips — yet scientific progress on that front is slow, so the only object that responds to their commands is me. Seriously though, if a kid shows zero gratitude, going on helping them can only aid their downfall.

5. *Kids are charming tyrants.* Original Sin applies to them too. Even if we'd like to grant every wish, we do no good by forgetting to impose limits. That's the big amnesia in modern culture, parents, and even schools — every educational platform, really. We need to show kids that limits don't sabotage them but save them; limits expand their freedom and pave the way to real happiness. As a friend says, children shouldn't be invisible, nor should they be invaders. They need a healthy dose of *affectionate neglect*.

6. *Kids must, in due time, obey, then detest, then reinvent their parents.* There comes a stage of "de-satellization" which we must not just accept but actually hope for.

7. *If you take care of someone else's kids, God takes care of yours.* Once, during my ninety-eighth novena for an issue affecting one of my children that just wouldn't budge, I got a plea for practical help (a mom who couldn't buy textbooks for her child). I helped — barely — and the long-awaited breakthrough happened. This truth is so real I'll say it again: if you look after other people's kids, God looks after yours.

Chapter Nine

Why Stay Married Even if ...
He Makes Me Suffer

When I dragged my future husband to a premarital course in Assisi, I ripped him away from a week in the snow, convinced that listening to a friar talk about love, couples, and the sacrament—alongside a hundred total strangers—would be far more intriguing than the ski slopes in Gressoney. Later on (much later), I discovered there was no greater nightmare for him. "Think how cold it is in the Aosta Valley," I'd say, "and how tedious putting on and taking off ski boots is, plus you'd have to do without me." (Personally, I'd only go skiing under some tyrannical regime that forced me there. And even then, I'd renounce basically anything to avoid it: if I must break a leg, I'd rather do it in the warmth.) Now that I know him much better, I can appreciate the heroism with which he sacrificed himself—without complaining too loudly, really. (Back then we were very polite fiancés; he'd yet to make it clear he hated any group that's more than, say, 1.5 people. Even when it's just the two of us, he thinks one person too many is in the room, unless I'm sleeping.) I had no clue how much I was risking by dragging him to an event full of other human beings—some of them friars, and none with a D-cup. I suspect he seriously considered abandoning me in Assisi so he could go marry a sturdy, rosy-cheeked Alpine farmgirl (or even a cow, in a pinch) just so he could stay in peace on his beloved snow.

Blessed Is the Day We "Got It Wrong"

Anyway, he always says he should have realized from the start that I was the kind of person you steer clear of—like on our very first date, when I announced I wanted a car big enough for strollers. But to me, that Assisi retreat sounded like the most beautiful place on Earth, and I had no inkling how utterly uninterested he was. I'm sharing this slightly off-topic memory (straying off topic is my specialty) as part of my future monument to the "unknown husband" that I plan to erect one day—a glass-concrete statue of a man slumped over. It'll be dedicated to all spouses left waiting outside dressing rooms for hours with no provisions, dragged to IKEA, or deported to prayer meetings.

What makes it worse is that besides subjecting my husband to cruelty and "violence against men" (forcing him to trade a weekly ski pass for a silly wooden name tag that read "GUIDO—ROME"), I realize I actually got very little out of that premarital course at the time. I listened to Fr. Giovanni, who spoke about the "nuclei of death" for couples, with this blasé superiority, certain none of that would ever apply to us. Not *us*, because we truly loved each other, and we were perfect together. (Or rather, I was perfect; he was workable, but obviously subject to my improvements.) Why on earth should I bother hearing about mortal threats to a relationship?

Luckily for me, I was an academic type who took pages and pages of notes with the same zeal that once drove me, before moving out, to copy down every recipe from my mother's day planner. (Though later I discovered the only real necessity in the kitchen is a good pair of reading glasses so you can see how long to nuke your prepackaged meals. The instructions are printed in some microscopic font designed to taunt you: "You don't just fail at cooking, you're also old, nyah nyah.") Unlike all those recipes, though, the notes from that course turned out to be incredibly useful. I've reread them multiple times, for all the dangers we've encountered or likely will—because not only are we *not* the perfect couple, we're actually quite normal, maybe even sub-normal, to be honest. I've also used what I learned to make sense of other people's marriages. Everything Fr. Giovanni said turned out to be prophetic.

When he talked about a couple's "failure to detach" from their families of origin as a lethal threat, he wasn't overstating. I know people who, even though they've started a new family, still live the life chosen by their old one, by their parents: they live in a house owned by their relatives, work in a "family business" they never really wanted, and are overshadowed by overbearing parents. They might also be missing out on the chance to test themselves in the real world. That confrontation with reality—shared struggles and all—is a huge privilege, though there are times you'd happily skip it (like paying your kids' dentist and then realizing your shopping spree is off this year). But needing to "obey circumstances" is precious; it schools us, keeps us grounded. ("Lord God, give me a reason to get out of bed." "You're broke.") It teaches us to follow the woodgrain of reality, which is not a product of our imagination but a solid truth that sometimes we run smack into, quite painfully.

Of course, everything's relative: in Beverly Hills last week, a woman felt "poor" because on Thursday she had to clean her kitchen herself; I know people who act as if they're cursed by fate if their maid quits right before a trip to the Côte d'Azur; meanwhile, there are folks who *are* the maid.

Giulia, I can't say it right to your face that you're a bit spoiled and not great at your job. That if you weren't your father's daughter, they wouldn't even let you make photocopies in that office—at best you'd serve as a decorative potted banana plant. (It's not that you're incompetent; you just aren't cut out for that work.) At the very least, though, *don't* complain that you wish you got more help from your parents. Actually, you should be getting *less* help: go pick a place in the outskirts, deal with a mortgage, choose the wrong bathroom tiles, meet your deadlines, skip calling a babysitter so you find yourself washing your hair at 3 a.m. between bouts of puke, decide between eating out or buying a new sweater. All these are small "trials," sure, but trials nonetheless on the path toward full independence from your family of origin—which maybe helped you a ton financially and with property, making it that much harder to break free. It's even tough for your closest friends to say anything to you about it, because you're stuck in this intense dynamic of parental interference—psychological, maybe financial—and from the outside, it's hard to give advice without cutting the branch your friend is perched on.

That said, countless people fail to emancipate from their parents *even if* they never got help. The imprinting and conditioning of one's birth family can be insanely powerful, sometimes downright mystifying. How does that dull, somewhat selfish mother— who, let's face it, is also frumpy and overweight—manage to keep her children under her thumb, adored by them, whereas my kids see it as their personal mission to tank my self-esteem? (I'll admit, I'm envious. My darling kids think anyone interested in what I type on my computer late at night must have serious mental-health issues, and if I attempt to voice a thought out loud, they immediately jab up the volume on their AirPods.) Probably we can't fully grasp the unique patterns of every family system (some people truly need a professional!). But I do know that once you form a new family, the old family should step back and keep pushing the spouses toward each other, never barging in with judgments or sneaky, manipulative criticisms (the specialty of certain controlling mothers).

The key to freeing yourself from your family of origin is learn-ing to *disappoint* your parents. When Jesus says, "Whoever loves father or mother more than me is not worthy of me," He's speaking also about a newly formed family: the new partnership between spouses must trump every other bond. Often, however, at least one spouse can't sever that umbilical cord—further complicated by financial or practical dependence ("All muscled up, but still needs Mom to peel his pistachios ..."). Nor can we allow our-selves—though we may be tempted—to let the grandparents raise the grandchildren, potentially doing for them or for their own children what they never afforded themselves. Yes, their motives may be good, wanting to shield their kids and grandkids from struggles and suffering. But it's the children's right to face difficul-ties. And about mother-son relationships, I plead the Fifth, as both a daughter-in-law and a future mother-in-law to that hussy who'll one day steal away my baby. (Future fiancée, you know who you are—I'm joking, I adore you.)

Then there are other "nuclei of death" I've seen often. For example, one spouse is married to his job: it might start as a genuine survival need for the family but becomes a slavish idol, more important than family life. Eventually you find yourself widowed *within* a marriage that isn't what you hoped. Once more, everything's relative: some dads think "a bit of security" means being able to pay for college; others assume it means three houses per kid plus a mini factory for each. Families break over money; sometimes they never reconcile, not even at a funeral. Indeed, those who aren't sure they'll meet the Father afterward often grow even more embittered in the face of death. Money, Fr. Emidio used to say, is like an oak that plants itself in your heart's center. As it grows, it chokes out everything else. By contrast, being insecure financially is an uncomfortable place, but at least the precarious pray for real, because that prayer is the lifeline to their survival.

In any case, the things we've discussed so far are within the realm of "serious but treatable" couple maladies—something you can cure with the right "medicine": a spiritual mentor (if possible), a life of faith, prayer, as many sacraments as feasible, maybe a community or circle of friends who can support and correct you if needed (like the buddy who punches you when you're tempted to cheat on your wife).

But over the years, I've also encountered couples in need of immediate "hospitalization," so to speak—stories that left me thinking, "No, please, I refuse to believe it's possible. This can't be real." And yet it was. Stories where you think, "Okay, folks, this is rock-bottom. You can't go any lower than that." But since the human heart is an abyss, you *can* always sink deeper. Men who kept a second home and a second wife in another city. Spouses who racked up hidden debts, mortgaged properties without the other knowing, faked degrees and job titles. Gambling addictions, substances of every kind, a string of lies that followed. Serial cheating—both sides—some guys had "the other woman" and also "the other man," and some wives had "another man" plus "another woman," or you'd see the oh-so-upstanding educator or prominent teacher who, after sleeping with every female in his village, moved on to the trans scene in the city next door. Or a spouse who'd experienced childhood abuse and eventually couldn't handle sex anymore, leaving the other to wait patiently for years without any intimacy (which is way more common than people think, for an astonishing variety of reasons), until they snapped and became the reigning sadomasochist king or queen of the local nightlife. Secret abortions that carved out an unbridgeable gulf of pain (and even when abortions are shared decisions, they often leave nearly fatal wounds). Husbands who lost their jobs and decided they were unworthy, shutting out their wives—and wives who decided, "Right, *now* it's my time," throwing themselves insanely into fitness at forty, plus fancy gear, diets, near-Olympic training (when, realistically, they might place fourth in a local race), dumping kids and blameless husbands behind (again: see that monument I mentioned). And you can swap the roles—sometimes it's the woman who deserves the statue.

So here's the question: *What do we do when our suffering comes directly from marriage itself?* Is there a point when it's legitimate to walk away?

I feel—speaking ever so carefully, with respect for those carrying big crosses, and for those (really everyone) dealing with the daily burdens of keeping it all together—that the real turning point is learning to see these snags *not* as the problem but as the *solution*. Lots of folks stay resentful their whole lives over something that derailed their plan. But the key is realizing that we ourselves are always the problem. That changes everything. The cross—even the "unfair" one caused by another person's wrongdoing—is not the enemy but the path. All the work I can do is on my own conversion, not on changing others or altering reality.

We each have a side that's public, visible to others; a side we alone see; and a side only the Lord sees. *That* is the issue: we're blind to our own real problem, but it gets revealed by doing what we're called to do—like staying with our spouse and kids, our family, first of all. Whenever something really wears us down, it's telling us something crucial about ourselves.

A friar once said that in every movie, there's a hero and there's an antagonist. In our life story (since faith is the story of our journey into death), *we* are the antagonist, even though we prefer playing the hero. We might sometimes look saintly, but we're structurally two-faced; let someone step on our toe, and we explode. (Apparently, St. Francis didn't respond the way I do—yelling "You deserve the ugliest demise, you sniveling grub!"—when someone stole his parking space. I've at least learned "kid-friendly" insults now that I have children, like "He neither works nor sweats nor fights, and he's got a mother who's a floozy," a relic of my old soccer-fan days in Curva Nord.[34]) It's shocking how much nastiness can pour out of my heart at certain times, even when I thought I was sort of good. We're not responsible for this two-faced nature, which St. Paul in Romans 7 describes so perfectly ("I do the evil I don't want to do"); it's just how deeply wounded we are by sin. All we can do—through a faith-filled life—is chip away at the power of that side we so easily see in others but rarely spot in ourselves.

The difficulties we face, even in our families, are golden opportunities for our salvation.

So it's not really about begging a "favor" from God or, in dire situations, a miracle. It's about realizing we can become Jesus Christ and even mediate for those around us. We can do something, change things, grow up. If we absorb mean words, grumbles, if we share our money and time, if we stay in an absurd situation without going berserk, then we reshape ourselves at the deepest level. Saints are those (few) who truly change in life.

At the heart of it all is that *death is a passage to salvation*. We convert when we see someone else being martyred, just as others are convinced when they see *us* let ourselves be ground down for real—and not just in words, like me. (Hence, I pray no one ever interviews the husband of that rumored "submissive wife.")

---

[34] "Curva Nord" refers to the north-side stand of the AC Milan soccer (football) stadium, where the most vocal and passionate fans, known as "ultras," sit.

A confessor once said to me, "Ask your kids what they think of you, and then confess *that*." But I'm too scared. (Though I know what they think of my books: "Among a trillion monkeys randomly typing on a computer, one might produce *The Divine Comedy*. For a Fabio Volo[35] book, twenty-seven. One by Mom? 100 billion.") Still, the holy Curé d'Ars once asked Jesus to show him his own soul, and the horror nearly killed him — so at least I'm consoled.

Basically, humanity is split. By embracing our vocation and offering our lives, we unify ourselves. In marriage, as you unite with someone else, you unite within yourself — and that movement can become a kind of horizontal transcendence, if not vertical. Entering that process means the cross, with all its mystery, is no longer an obstacle; it no longer makes you say, "I married the wrong person." In that mystery, which might be genuine suffering as well as the tightrope act of holding everything together, you see the cross is unsolvable unless you pick it up. We won't get "justice" for the wrong we've endured, so we might as well come to terms with that. Without the cross, we're hateful to each other. Even Jesus, though he was God's Son, learned obedience through suffering; we, on the other hand, want everything from God as long as He spares us the cross.

The cure for all neuroses is whether we want a personal relationship with Jesus or not. Most of us couldn't care less about access to God; we don't center Him in our hearts — the same God that Jews dare not name except once a year to the sound of drums. Meanwhile, we get to call Him "Dad," "Papa," we can pull on His ears, eat from His plate, yet we remain uninterested in Emmanuel, God-with-us. Instead, we need a truly personal relationship with

[35] Italian author.

the Lord: radical, total, uncompromising. We must keep asking to know His will—it's not as easy to discern or to do as some claim. We need to do constant acts of love to show God we're serious. And when He's convinced, He comes to us, treats us as friends, entrusts us with those dearest to Him. He becomes the Spouse of our soul, a traveling companion.

Marriage isn't a job—it's a workshop. Living in close quarters with other people is heavy at times, downright unbearable at others. The cross is going toward the other even when they're unpleasant, coexisting with the tangles because that's how the family endures. We *need* those tangles to press on and to develop empathy; tangles keep us from always looking perfect. The Incarnation is about submitting to the slow torture of daily life and mediocrity, all while staying rooted in praise (yes, that's the secret). Accept what you dislike—this "passive" cross—and accept you're just a creature. We're layered like a club sandwich—Fr. Emidio's image, which I find brilliantly descriptive. We're not straightforward; we're all "I'd like to … I don't want to … but if you want." Embracing reality heals those contradictions, unifying us. Then we can walk our faith journey seriously. And since the Lord is a *person*—truly a person—if we say, "Change me, break open my mind, convert me," He does. The dysfunctional side of us is held in check by accepting suffering, not by trying to dodge it. "So it is no longer I who live, but Christ who lives in me." Only that wins the human drama.

When you meet Him, you're happy. The main thing is not to compromise but to risk it all. We need to grasp how huge the stakes are—eternity. Sin always grows from our infantile side; we're stuck on trivialities, missing what's crucial. Our marital status matters less than sharing the experience. The hardest conversion isn't from Islam, or Freemasonry, or any external "enemy"; the hardest conversion is from stupidity, from warm milk, from "I feel / I don't feel," from chasing gratification.

Are we willing to be crucified by our spouse's flaws? If we remain, we admit our strength can't fix reality. Otherwise, we boil with anger and frustration over everything that's missing — affection, time, alignment with our expectations.

According to Tolkien, the most beautiful marriages are those marked by limits, the ones that, by demanding work, demand a more radical conversion — conversion to Christianity, which doesn't exorcise death but tells you if you lose your life for others, you rise again. Staying in communion when it's not easy, surrendering your ego — that's holiness. Conversion means taking responsibility for others, so, in tough relationships, we keep asking, "What would Jesus do?" Would He blow up because the house is a mess, or say nothing, or try a gentle word? Figuring that out isn't always simple: faith is as precise as a phone number — mess up one digit, and you're off. It isn't like lasagna, where if you use a little less parmesan, it's still lasagna. (Credit again to Fr. Emidio.) So read the Gospel and ask, "What would Jesus do here? What would the saints do?" Once the Lord sees we truly want to do what's right, *He* can work the miracle in a heartbeat. Because He isn't just a friend — He's the Almighty walking alongside us, pushing in the same direction, working for our happiness even more than we do.

His goal is to capture our hearts so we convert and learn to serve. He wants us to rise, because we *can* rise! The one crucified is the Lion of Judah. So the cross isn't the problem — it's how we heal our problems.

When a major trial hits, let's remember the Lord is opening the way to eternal life. Jesus is alive, and those who follow Him won't die!

Ultimately, eternal life is decided right there with the diapers at home and with the people who wear us out. Family life denies our ego. It constantly offers us chances to shoulder one another's burdens. We carry a ton of those burdens, but then we ruin it all with anger or gossip. Humility, kindness, goodness—that is how to be "the stone rejected." Love, gentleness, forgiveness, yielding, patience; being a bit foolish, handling the everyday chores as well.

If we let ourselves get ground up, there's hope. Because in this world there are bad people and people who just don't get caught. We're all pitiful creatures. Words can camouflage and confuse, but in reality, we're all dwarfs on stilts. Yet having patience for others makes us dear to God. Then we meet Him and experience fullness.

And when we meet Him, we can't help wanting to love Him with all our heart, soul, mind, and strength. Meaning with our *heart*, i.e., setting our commitments in the right order; with our *soul*, i.e., dedicating time to Him; with our *strength*, i.e., using our resources, money included, in His service; and with our *mind*, i.e., applying all our intelligence—like we would if we had a life-threatening illness, seeking the best doctor, informing ourselves, putting in the time, trying to figure out what to do. For us, the "plague" we need to survive is our muddled mind. God asks us to use our brains—He gave them to us!—so we can experience fullness, meet Him fully in the present, in the simplest details of life.

At that point, we also become an anchor for others. When Jesus says, "I will make you fishers of men," His disciples don't get it, but they're crazy in love with Him and willing to do anything. When we latch on to God, we, too, can pull others out of the water without judging them, because He cares about everyone while they're alive. There's no need for fireworks: "Father, let them be one so the world may believe." We become one with someone when we agree to lose. Christianity's model is Christ's self-emptying: letting go, losing status. Only when you're so stripped down that you're left with nothing for yourself are you safe enough.

So truly, *blessed* is the struggle (big or small) we must face. Blessed is the day we got it wrong, because the more we lose, the more we cling to God.

Women's Decalogue

How to Choose the Perfect Foundation

There are about ten types of foundation, each with a different level of coverage—from BB cream to stick foundations, through fluids, illuminating finishes, tanning formulas, and so-called "treatment" products. Let's go through them one by one.

So, BB cream is the least covering option.

Now that all the men have stopped reading (to encourage them to skip straight to the last page, which I have titled "A Tactical Analysis of Sacchi's AC Milan" or "Give It to Her and Be Submissive"), we can talk among ourselves, ladies. Because this chapter is strictly off-limits to men. (If my typical reader were my husband, I could title it "Honey, We Need to Talk," and he'd immediately toss the whole book into the trash.)

In reality, I just want to share, with my fellow women, ten "maintenance rules" for marriage—ones that (acknowledging specifics, differences, and exceptions) I believe can help us avoid even getting close to crisis mode, that point at which you might say, "I'll stay anyway, even if ..."

These rules are off-limits to men because, let's be honest, *we* set the tone in the home, the climate of the relationship (though no need to publicize that too much). We don't have to share with our husband *all* the personal work we're doing on ourselves—just (hopefully) the end result.

Blessed Is the Day We "Got It Wrong"

We don't give life only when we give birth: we give life in many circumstances, every day. We have a vital function that goes beyond ourselves, radiating all around us. For instance, our mood weighs heavily on the entire family, for better or worse. Once we have people depending on us, we can't afford plunges into deep sadness, nor can we do those teenage meltdown stunts only our old squad of girlfriends could calm us down from. Our impact on our partner and our kids can extend way beyond our intentions. Plus, women come equipped with a powerful toolset that lets us, say, decode an adolescent daughter's mood from the single tone in which she says "yeah," while Dad is still switching on the audio channel—really hoping that at least she's not talking *to* him. It's that onboard system that can let us—if we use it maliciously—zero in on a man's vulnerabilities to make him do exactly what we want, and he'll never suspect a thing.

Hence, this chapter is forbidden to men because *we* need to grasp these points first, and we don't necessarily need to clue them in on all the introspection we decide to do about ourselves.

If something is wearing us down in our marriage, our only move is to start by changing ourselves. Sure, the expectation—call it a hope, not a demand, because love is the opposite of possessiveness—is that our husband might also change. And change (almost) certainly will arrive, because a man cannot hold out against a woman who respects him, honors him, truly loves him and his freedom, and nudges him to raise his gaze higher. At that point, he'll choose to emerge from his cave (be it work, the couch, sports, or his private bubble) to be with her, because being with her—once a woman gives up her demands—becomes paradise.

For a woman, this means giving up something: her will to dominate (whether she does so explicitly or through manipulation). For a man, it means *adding* something—overcoming self-centeredness

164

and starting to give in a manly and free way, not just putting up with it or acting resigned, but taking real pleasure in making his woman happy. I've never seen a man start to add that "something" if the woman beside him hasn't first carved out a space for him.

So how do we create that space?

Well, if I had the foolproof answer, I'd have written a *New York Times* bestseller. I'd have a husband head-over-heels for me, calling me for no other reason than to chat (rather than just telling me where he parked the car), coming home and hanging out in whatever room I'm in after asking, "How's it going?" (Okay, fine, it's happened that he actually listened to my response—but both times I was in my underwear.) The truth is, I don't really know. All I know is that we can only make ourselves more lovable and work on ourselves, starting with small daily steps. Here, I've tried to list some fixed points—things I find helpful to recall many times a day. I say "recall" because I'm the first to forget them with embarrassing ease. Whatever my husband does, I tend to think I should show him how to do it *properly* (just imagine how that makes me irresistible in his eyes), as in: actually, the shoes need to go on the second shelf; the prosciutto should have been San Daniele, and only 200 grams, because it spoils in the fridge; plus, sure, that sweater's cute, but it's not as flattering as the one I got you. I think my all-time record was complaining that the mattress protector was too rumpled on his side of the bed: "So, now you're telling me I can't even sleep the way I want?" And yet he didn't give me the tongue-lashing that I arguably deserved.

Given my despairing situation, I have to add a disclaimer I should repeat after every line—but to spare us the tedium, I'll say it just once (please keep it in mind all the way through): *I'm incapable of living out everything I'm about to say*, at least not the way I'd like. I'm not sure if I preach well, but I definitely practice poorly. I'm forever fighting that urge to control and reshape my husband—and most of the time, that urge gets its way. If you doubt it, just ask him—but I say that lightly, because he never responds to questions that might spark conversation. Not unless they contain certain magic phrases like "Confederations Cup" or "intelligence services." ("How are you feeling?" is definitely not one of those phrases. In fact, they say asking a man about his emotional state is like asking a woman how much she weighs.)

One last caution: men can skip this chapter (we've established that) along with any woman who:

- Never feels superior to her husband
- Never criticizes him
- Doesn't constantly say, "See? I was right" (I might as well have "I told you so" tattooed on my biceps)
- Doesn't think "everything would be better if he finally did it my way"
- Doesn't try to monitor everything he does, who he talks to, where he goes
- Doesn't see him as just one more of her children
- Trusts him
- Knows how to carve out time for herself because she lets him handle many things—even if he does them differently than she would have
- Always receives his gifts with gratitude
- Knows how to express her own needs and vulnerabilities
- Doesn't think she should carry most of the big tasks alone (educating the kids, handling finances, making major decisions)
- Is naturally all these things, without chemical assistance

How to Choose the Perfect Foundation

First step: be quiet. Talk as little as possible. Over time, this can become a habit—or at least something you don't have to bite your tongue so hard to achieve. Try it for a month. Some say that after two or three days it gets easier (not in my experience, but I've never lasted three days), and regardless, don't give up if you slip up—just start over with humility and determination. For thirty days, do your absolute best not to express a single criticism, no pointed remarks, no sarcastic jokes, *no commentary*. (Yes, even dirty looks count as criticism.) Nothing. Silence is like a detox diet for the soul. It has a cumulative effect: the more you keep silent, the more natural it becomes. It's like an exorcism. You'll discover it really wasn't necessary to highlight *everything*—or at least not right away. You're allowed to say positive things, but even those should be used sparingly, because sometimes even praise includes an unconscious criticism. For example, "I'm glad you finally changed those light bulbs I've been asking about" can subtly mean "You normally make me wait forever." "I'm glad you exercised today" can mean "You never do anything." "I'm happy you listened to me" can imply "I know how things should be, and congrats for doing it my way." Keeping silent has a remarkable effect on men: it frees their space, helps them bring out their best side. You should try to be silent even when something hurts you. Indeed, it may be in that very moment that silence works miracles. It breaks the cycle of argument, soothes the situation, encourages reflection. And when talking about others, the wonderful rule "if you can't say anything nice, say nothing" is a balm for the relationship. Being less hyper-critical shows your sweeter side to the man—the welcoming one he fell in love with. (A man marries a woman hoping she'll never change; a woman marries a man certain she'll change him.) Everyone can figure out a trick to help keep this commitment. For instance, jot down on a sticky note the things you want to say the moment they come into your head, and then hold off until the end of the day. It'll quickly fill up with futile little nitpicks ("Yes, the fork actually goes on the left, but apparently no one's died from creative place setting yet, honey."). In the middle you might spot a few truly important matters—ones that should be addressed, but not *at* the moment they happen. By day's end, reading over them, you'll see most of your "urgent corrections" were silly. The ones that really must be said are very few, and none need to be stated *when* they occur. I've tried it a few times, and by evening I felt deeply embarrassed by what I'd noted, scribbling furiously in my bossy-little-teacher mode—yet just hours later, it all seemed ridiculous.

Second step: adopt a positive bias toward the man. After a month of silence, it'll be a lot easier to say, "I'm on your side, I cheer for you. I know that if I make you feel loved, you'll do your best to love me back. I assume you're doing so, even if at first glance it doesn't seem that way. I mean, is it really possible that every time—every single time—I talk to you, honey, your gaze drifts off because you found a flake in the wall to fix?" Having a positive bias means accepting how he does things, respecting him, and starting from the assumption that you're not any better than he is. In the time it took to write these few lines, for instance, I fought the urge to tell my husband—who just heated a frozen pizza in the oven—that he picked the worst brand of pizza, used the wrong dish, and that cutting pizza with a wheel inevitably means touching it with your hands (which is strictly against my "operating-room" hygiene standards). Instead, I stayed quiet, and so far nobody has dropped dead. Of course, there's virtually nothing I'd do the same way he does it, but there are many ways to accomplish tasks. The more we accept his style, the faster he'll start asking our opinion. Unbelievable, but true—he will.

Third step: express our wishes simply, directly, minus demands, and with humility. A man who feels appreciated, valued, and respected will do *anything* to make us happy—provided we're not the ones telling him how. We can't micromanage him in this area too. The man doesn't "get" us, but he *can* learn us. We just have to speak straightforwardly about what we'd like, without fear or second-guessing—leaving him the freedom to disagree and, above all, the freedom to do what we want in his own time and manner. Then he can freely decide to do something for us (not because we "sold" him on it, but because he wants to give us a gift, even if he doesn't agree). "Don't you think we should go to that event?" isn't ideal. "I'd like to go because it interests me" instead expresses *my* need, leaving him free to disagree—and also free to do something for me just to make me happy. Often we're reluctant to ask for help—or we ask in a sneaky way that deprives the man of his free will—because we don't believe anyone can truly look after us or meet our needs (this can stem from personal or family history). But in marriage, we can be vulnerable, we can say something hurts us, we can admit we have needs. We can ask for help, as long as we accept the form it takes.

Fourth step: give up controlling his actions—the pinnacle of this journey. Your husband is not your child. It's a temptation we must fight. We think we're "helping," but he experiences it as control. And there's a dynamic I can't quite explain: the more we try to control a man, the more likely he is to do precisely what we've been criticizing him for. Letting go of that control can be dizzying—we're scared to release our grip, we have no idea what might happen—but the bonus is a far more satisfying sex life, because every criticism makes us more and more resemble his mother, and come on, who wants to be their mother-in-law? And more importantly, what man wants to sleep with his mother?

Blessed Is the Day We "Got It Wrong"

Sometimes, after years of us pushing our agenda, the man (who can lean toward laziness in relationships, "not dying for her") would rather keep delegating and let us decide. So if we stop controlling, he'll ask us what to do. We have to bounce it back, act like a rubber wall, let him know we really trust him, that *he* has to decide. We must persist. Act as if we trust him—because how we regard him transforms him.

Fifth step: remember that men express their needs through criticism. If a man criticizes you, he's asking for love, attention, respect—some acknowledgment. For example, men rarely say, "I wish you'd spend more time with me." They'll more likely say, "You devote too much time to the kids." "You always criticize me" means "I wish you'd encourage me more, make me feel more appreciated." We women critique men to educate or improve them; men aren't interested in that. They just want to be loved.

Sixth step: giving up criticizing him doesn't mean giving up on yourself. Quite the opposite—it means getting more from the relationship. And you mustn't give up something that's truly about you, so long as it doesn't deprive him or the family, or, obviously, put you in danger. We can learn to let go of controlling his mindset while still standing up for our own perspective on matters that directly concern us (like health, working hours, or personal time—assuming any is left), because only we know our true needs. With everything else, it takes an effort of trust, a leap of faith in him.

Seventh step: trusting him also means learning to be thankful for what we get—gifts, acts of service, kind words, attention. Critiquing a gift is strictly forbidden. I model this so well that I suspect my husband, resigned to always picking the "wrong" gift and hearing me point it out, might just stop gifting me anything at all.

Eighth step: do fun things together, find times for spiritual and intellectual nourishment, moments of recreation. Also, create empty spaces where you're together just for the pleasure of being in each other's company—something that, by step eight, we'll hopefully have relearned to appreciate. Breaking away from the hectic daily schedule may feel like "wasting time," when in fact it's time spent on what matters most.

Ninth step: find the time to take care of yourself. Learn how to say no (personally, a major problem), to rest, to preserve yourself. Figure out some small routine that soothes you, even if it's difficult during certain periods. But it should be treated as a family necessity, because a worn-out woman is likely to be resentful, definitely prone to complaining. "I don't have time" is never really true: time for ourselves is a primary duty, like brushing our teeth. (In my case, I go running every day, whenever I can fit it in, even before sunrise or near midnight—but people who know me claim I only do that because it's strenuous, so my internal Nazi commander gives me a pass.) By the same logic, maintaining at least a thin thread of contact with a friend is important—even if in certain years it might be really hard.

Tenth step: value their father in front of the children and ensure they respect him—or better, avoid undermining him, because it's natural for kids to respect Dad unless we push the other way. It's crucial to trust his parenting style, appreciate how *he's* the one who gets them to take off their cardigans, buys them plane tickets so they can fly off—basically, he's the one cutting the cord. We can be sure that his style, so different from ours, is an invaluable treasure for our kids.

Men's Decalogue

Deep Analysis of Football Playbook and Tactics

or rather Give It to Him
and Be Submissive

(Yes, I'm sure you'll read it now)

1. Listen to her.
2. Look at her (really try to notice if she trimmed her hair or is wearing a skirt).
3. Listen some more—another two minutes. You can do it.
4. Tell her she's beautiful. Maybe not as beautiful as Dybala, but close.
5. Defend her from herself, from her own mental hijinks.
6. Protect her from external threats.
7. Free her from useless burdens.
8. Guard your heart and your gaze for her alone.
9. Love your kids.
10. Be ready to die for her, one grocery cart at a time.

c

About the Author

Costanza Miriano is a wife and mother of four children. She works as a journalist for Rai (Italian public television), is a freelance writer on education and relationships, and has worked with the Pontifical Council for the Laity. She has a blog that has had more than three million readers in two years, and she has written four books, including *Marry Him and Be Submissive* and *Marry Her and Die for Her*, which have sold around seventy thousand copies in Italy and have been translated into ten languages, including Spanish, French, Portuguese, Polish, Slovenian, and now English.

Sophia Institute

Sophia Institute is a nonprofit institution that seeks to nurture the spiritual, moral, and cultural life of souls and to spread the gospel of Christ in conformity with the authentic teachings of the Roman Catholic Church.

Sophia Institute Press fulfills this mission by offering translations, reprints, and new publications that afford readers a rich source of the enduring wisdom of mankind.

Sophia Institute also operates the popular online resource CatholicExchange.com. *Catholic Exchange* provides world news from a Catholic perspective as well as daily devotionals and articles that will help readers to grow in holiness and live a life consistent with the teachings of the Church.

In 2013, Sophia Institute launched Sophia Teachers to renew and rebuild Catholic culture through service to Catholic education. With the goal of nurturing the spiritual, moral, and cultural life of souls, and an abiding respect for the role and work of teachers, we strive to provide materials and programs that are at once enlightening to the mind and ennobling to the heart; faithful and complete, as well as useful and practical.

Sophia Institute gratefully recognizes the Solidarity Association for preserving and encouraging the growth of our apostolate over the course of many years. Without their generous and timely support, this book would not be in your hands.

www.SophiaInstitute.com
www.CatholicExchange.com
www.SophiaTeachers.org